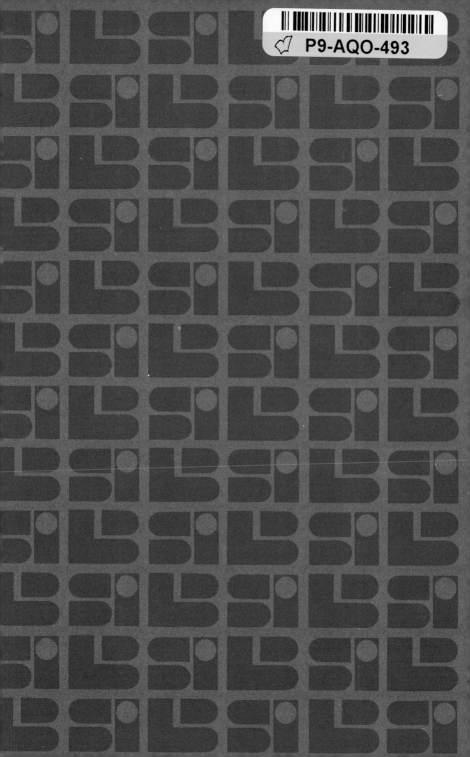

Capt. Samuel K. Earp

The Blue Water Bait Book

The Blue Water Bait Book

Secrets of Successful Big Game Fishing

Captain Samuel A. Earp
and
Captain William J. Wildeman

A SPORTS ILLUSTRATED BOOK

Little, Brown and Company — Boston — Toronto

FIRST EDITION

T 08/74

Unless otherwise noted, all the photographs are by Merrill Green
Photography, Juno, Florida. The photographs on pages 152–161
are by the authors. The drawings are by De Carter Art, Palm
Beach, Florida.

Library of Congress Cataloging in Publication Data

Earp, Samuel A
    The blue water bait book; secrets of successful big
game fishing.

    "A Sports illustrated book."
    1. Big game fishing. 2. Bait. I. Wildeman,
William J., joint author. II. Title.
SH457.5.E18   799.1'2   74-5273
ISBN 0-316-20330-0

Sports Illustrated Books
are published by
Little, Brown and Company
in association with
Sports Illustrated Magazine

*Published simultaneously in Canada
by Little, Brown & Company (Canada) Limited*

PRINTED IN THE UNITED STATES OF AMERICA

To those who know
and
to those about to learn
the skills of big game fishing

Contents

vii

Introduction

Twenty-five or thirty years ago big game fishing was almost the exclusive province of the professional boat captains and the very wealthy. Now it is open to anyone with a 20-foot or larger boat and the desire.

This book is designed to give you the *how to* and, just as important, the *why* of what has been learned in more than two decades of professional big game fishing experience.

For those men and women who have tried to but never have caught a marlin or sailfish, or for those whose catches are poor year after year, the reason is generally in underestimating the importance in processing, rigging, and presenting the bait. If nothing else consider that you must first raise the fish and make him "eat" before there is any chance of hooking and landing him — and this depends on the bait alone!

At the same time much of the money spent on bait is wasted through not knowing how to rig and care for it. It is easy to see that, exclusive of tackle, bait alone is expensive, running from a few dollars up to $10 or even $40 for a day's fishing, depending on the type of bait used. For example, ballyhoo is usually sold at about $2 a dozen, and marlin bait from $10 to $40 a dozen. For the avid angler this can mean hundreds of dollars spent each year on blue water bait alone.

As in other professions, big game fishermen swap their knowledge of baits and rigs, and the like. In this sense we are indebted to our friends in the Bahamas, the Gulf ports and the Florida Keys, and farther north through to Ocean City, Brielle, Montauk, and "P" town. Many of these men have their favorite rigs. Some will have opinions that differ from ours. It is always wise to listen to them and then make up your own mind.

Only the spendthrifts and the most stubborn of men would not take time to listen to such professionals as Captain Fred Hastings, Captain Fred Voss, Jr., Charlie Hayden, Jack Conners, Captain Bill Black and his father, Captain Ken Black, Mutt Coble, Captain Roy Bosche, Bob Lewis, John and Paul Mumford, and others.

We believe we have included everything you need to hunt the big ones successfully. As far as possible, each section is complete in itself; that is, if you are going after sailfish simply turn to the right page and you will find out where to find them and how to troll for them. Effective big game baits and their advantages are listed under mullet, ballyhoo, squid, mackerel, etc. Other chapters include rigging basics, the care and freezing of bait, live baiting, and angling techniques.

Some skeptics will argue that all you need to do is throw some bait overboard with a hook and you'll catch fish. And it's true that some fish are so hungry they will eat anything, and have! Large dolphin have gobbled potato chips thrown overboard, and a sailfish once tried to eat a cotton swab dragged over the side. It's the ones that aren't bent on suicide this book is designed to put on the end of your line.

From a survey of many books on big game fishing, we find this is the only one written by professional fishermen. It shows how we fish for a living and will definitely increase your chances of taking big game fish anyplace in the world. And this book will save you time and money.

We are proud that this is the most accurate and complete book on blue water trolling baits ever published.

The Blue Water
Bait Book

1.

It's All in the Bait and the Way You Use It

At the outset there are some general principles which apply to all bait from mullet to squid, whether trolled shallow or deep, from rigger or flat line.

The cardinal rule of trolling is NEVER LET YOUR BAIT SPIN. A spinning bait results from incorrect rigging, bad bait, weeds on the bait or all three. Proper rigging of the bait is essential to (1) capturing the fish, (2) the length of time the bait will last when trolled, and (3) protecting your line from unraveling or snarling.

All blue water trolling bait is rigged either to swim

or skip, and is either trolled long or short; and on swimming baits, trolled either shallow or deep.

While it is true that bait and rigged bait from Florida has been shipped to Nova Scotia, Mexico, the Bahamas and as far away as Mexico and Panama, it is best to use bait that is local. This is because migrating big game fish change their feeding habits as they travel, depending on the bait available in a given area. As a result you will find the professional fishermen of Florida use a lot more mullet and ballyhoo, for instance, than squid and eels, which are popular farther north. The second and more important reason, however, is that your bait must be *fresh*; and locally processed bait has a much better chance of meeting this all-important requirement. When we use the term *fresh* we are including frozen bait when properly processed.

In order to be classed as *fresh frozen*, all bait when caught must be iced down immediately, or put in a chilling, but not freezing, brine. The care and handling of bait is covered in some detail in Chapter 3, but here we want to underline the principle that *any* bait you use must be either fresh or fresh frozen. If the bait is left in the sun before processing, freezer burned, or carelessly handled, you are going to catch far fewer fish. Certain fish such as billfish will sometimes hit a bad bait, then knock it off the hook; whereas with good, tough bait the same fish has been known to hit the bait repeatedly, giving the angler up to three or four, or even ten chances to hook the one he's worked so hard to raise. The other advantage is that with properly processed bait you don't have to change it as often, and remember, every time your bait is out of the water you decrease your chances of hooking a fish. You save money, too. With bad bait you will buy from three to five times as much, simply because it "washes out" much more quickly.

4

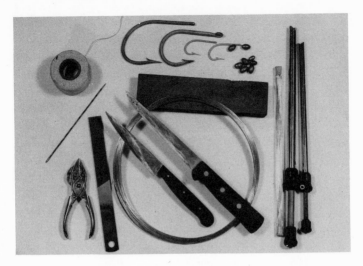

Basic equipment for rigging baits.

As you go through the chapters on specific baits, and as you actually use them, you will learn that each has its own lasting characteristics. For example, when you can get fresh ballyhoo, it is always preferable to frozen. Fresh frozen mullet is the choice over fresh, if properly processed, i.e., chilled, plugged, deboned, brined, and then frozen and so forth (the exception being fresh caught, cut and brined; then rigged and trolled).

Your local bait and tackle dealer is not only a good source of dependable and well-processed bait, but he can also fill you in on new as well as local variations in rigs. Almost every year there is some variation on proven rigs used the year before that outproduces the ones used the previous season. For instance, triple hooking your bait with swivels linking the hooks together for kingfish is new in recent years, as are umbrella rigs for striped bass and bluefish in New Jersey and New York. Changes have also occurred in the type of teasers used. Possibly 30 percent of the Florida sportfishing boats now carry daisy chains of plastic squids for teasers where they were almost unheard of eight or ten years ago, although they had been used successfully from Ocean City to Nova Scotia long before this. These examples are used just to point out again that your local bait and tackle dealer can, and will, go a long way to put the odds in your favor for a mount, a record, or simply improving your catch.

EQUIPMENT	TYPE	SIZE
Ballyhoo wire	copper	standard
Cooler	styrofoam	large
Deboners	stainless steel	proper
Gloves	cotton	to fit
Hooks	ring eye and needle eye	6/0–14/0
Hook file	flat bastard	standard
Knives	narrow blade filet	5″ 8″–9″
Leader wire	tinned or stainless	Nos. 6–15
Leads	egg shape	1/8–3 oz.
Linen thread*	medium weight	spool
Plastic bags	any	medium
Plastic bucket	any	regular
Pliers	Sportmate	small or large
Sewing needles	standard	5″
Snaps	stainless	assortment
Swivels		assortment
Whetstone	any	medium

NOTE: All equipment is not needed on any given bait. What you will need is listed under each specific bait.

* Waxed line or dental floss may be substituted.

2.

Basic Equipment for Rigging Bait

The equipment you'll need for the caring and rigging of trolling bait from the leader down is listed on the opposite page. It is essentially complete, and is basic to the well-equipped sportfishing boat. Where certain brand names are mentioned it is only what we prefer and in no way should limit your choice of any good quality equipment.

Leaders

When it comes to leaders there are several factors to be considered: (1) whether to use tinned (music) wire or coffee-colored stainless wire, (2) whether to use an all-wire leader, or a combination of wire and mono, or all monofilament.

Tinned wire will corrode and rust unless you spray it with CRC or WD-40; always wash it off with fresh water after a day's fishing. On the other hand, stainless will not rust but it will stretch, which means after one or two good fish it will curl and have to be thrown away.

But the main difference is that tinned wire has more strength for the same diameter. This means that you can substitute, for example, a #6 tinned wire for a #8 stainless without losing strength.

Some anglers prefer to use about 12 feet of mono attached to 2 or 3 feet of wire, particularly on sailfish. The reasons generally given for this type of leader are: (1) they are easier to handle, and (2) you can store more made-up rigs in a smaller area. And in the case of tournament release fishing, you can break light wire off more quickly. Also, the shorter the wire the less the chances of kinking. But be careful; mono will fray and break on the bill of a fish just as easily as wire will kink. This is especially true of any billfish that has been on a long time.

Hooks

The preferred hook is the galvanized one; they don't rust as quickly. Stainless hooks won't rust either, but believe it or not they're softer and tend to straighten out on a heavy fish, particularly when the hook does not have a complete bite in his mouth or jaw.

The following suggestions on size and quantity will be easy on your wallet and yet fill the basic requirements.

Size

6/o — get a dozen for use on very small bait, like 5- to 7-inch-long finger mullet.

7/o–8/o — get at least a dozen of each size. This is almost a universal hook for sailfish, dolphin, kingfish, bonito, etc.

9/o–14/o — get an assortment of these but not over a half dozen of any one size. Large hooks like these that are of top quality such as Martu, Sobey, Sea Demon and Seamate can run up to 50 cents each.

On your smaller-size hooks (6/o and 7/o), get a combination of needle eye and ring eye. This is suggested for several reasons. For instance, a needle eye hook is always preferred on ballyhoo. A ballyhoo has a narrow head to begin with and rigging with a ring eye often pushes the gills out slightly. When double hooking, if you use a combination of a ring eye and a needle eye you'll save a great deal of time. On some brands the eye of the hook is welded shut, so you have to use a needle eye with it for double hooking.

Whenever possible use short shank hooks for live baiting. There is less hardware showing and your rig is better because you don't have all that "iron" hanging out of your bait.

For head rigs use either a hook with a steep bite or one with a straight bite, both short shank. Since the whole hook is showing in a head rig you really don't need to be worried about the bite. About the only advantage of the steep bite hook is that it is much harder for the fish to throw once he's hooked.

In the belly rigs that follow, straight bite hooks should be used simply because they have more bite showing.

Hook Files

For a hook file all you need is a flat bastard scraper file, like the kind you use to file paint scrapers.

Move the file only one way, that is, against the serrations on the file. You are going to want a triangular or knife edge on your hooks, not a needle point. If you try and set your hook in a fish with a bony mouth, and it has a needle point, often it will bend and not penetrate.

Pliers

When it comes to fishing pliers the Sportmate brand is clearly the first choice. The size is up to the angler, but a pair in good condition is essential to rigging bait, so keep them well oiled. If they freeze up use some CRC or WD-40 penetrating oil. If they become really stuck then use a little Comet cleaner and work back and forth until free, then wash off, dry and oil.

Knives

Start with two, one with a short (5-inch), narrow blade for cutting and gutting. The Forschner is an excellent choice for this knife. Then get a regular fillet knife with a 6- to 9-inch medium-weight blade.

Deboners

Deboners come in five sizes, with the size depending entirely on the diameter. Always buy stainless steel deboners. Don't mess with aluminum deboners because they don't hold an edge and will bend. The slight extra cost for a stainless deboner is well worth the money.

Always keep your deboner sharp by using a rat-tail file on the inside cutting edge; trim burr off the outside with your hook file.

Sewing Thread

Buy plain linen thread or dental floss. Avoid dacron and monofilament because they slip; regular cotton thread is too weak in small diameter sizes. If you must use dacron or nylon, then wax it with beeswax.

Bait Sewing Needles

Bait sewing needles run from 3 to 10 inches in length. A good all around size is 5 inches.

Egg Sinkers

There are few things as irritating as picking up an egg sinker for rigging and finding the hole down the center is closed tight. When buying leads make sure that you look at each one; it takes just a minute and will save you time later on. Get an assortment of sizes from ⅛ to 3 ounces. Get a few "lunker" leads, and if you are going to hunt tuna you will need some in the 4- to 8-ounce category.

Snaps and Swivels

When buying snaps and swivels, buy Pompanette brand or any good stainless steel. Also, some fishermen prefer ball-bearing swivels when using spoons or rigging teasers.

Pompanettes are sized by the fish you are after, that is, "dolphin," "sailfish," "marlin," "tuna," and so forth. Buy an assortment. Be sure to carry some black swivels to be used when mackerel and kingfish fishing because these two fish especially will hit a shiny swivel and cut your line.

Two Other Thoughts

A good whetstone is a must to keep your knives razor sharp. Clorox is a must for use as an antiseptic, and for cleaning gloves, rags, etc.

3.

The Care and Freezing of Bait

Many anglers will invest in good baits and know how to rig the baits they are going to use and yet still do not understand the art of the caring and freezing of bait or how to keep it fresh on board.

The basic equipment is simply a well-insulated styrofoam cooler large enough to handle both the amount of bait you intend to carry plus the size of the individual baits themselves. By well-insulated we mean the thicker the styrofoam the better (an inch or more). Spend a few extra dollars for a good cooler to protect what you have already spent on bait.

A few simple rules will insure the color, appearance, and toughness of your bait:

1. If possible, thaw your bait the night before by leaving it on the ice in your cooler. This is the best method and what we call "natural" thawing.

2. Whether thawing your bait or keeping rigged bait iced down, make sure the drain at the bottom of the cooler is open at all times. The idea is to keep the bait cool — not to soak it in melted ice water.

3. If you can't thaw your bait "naturally," then thaw it in salt water before you start rigging.

We rate natural thawing the best method, saltwater next and finally, freshwater. Never thaw by leaving bait in the sun, or using an oven, etc. Layer your bait when packing in a cooler. Any bait, fresh or fresh frozen, should be layered in your cooler, that is, a layer of ice on the bottom then a layer of bait, then ice, bait, ice, bait, etc. An additional benefit of layering is being able to keep your rigged baits separate and ready for use. Put your unrigged baits on the lower layers or to one side.

When packing your rigged baits, make sure the wire ends are out of the ice. Ice will stick to the leaders and you want to avoid this. Place some damp newspapers under the leader wires only.

Make sure that your layers are even by reversing rigged ends and newspaper; that is, one layer of rigged baits and newspaper on the left; next layer, rigged ones and newspaper on the right, and so forth. In this way you will keep your bait neat and ready to use.

Remember that when you are raising fish, efficiency counts. Many an angler has hurriedly reached into his cooler to change or replace a bait and has come up with five or six tangled rigs, so be neat about it.

If traveling for an extended period of time where you must carry enough bait for a week or so, you can pack it in your styrofoam cooler, keeping it frozen with dry ice. However, make sure the bait is packed in plastic bags and the dry ice is covered with newspapers so the bait doesn't burn.

Freezer burn, whether from dry ice or the freezing compartment of your refrigerator, is the result of extreme cold coming into direct contact with the bait. The skin of the fish dries out and tears easily when trolled, so avoid using "burned" bait whenever possible. Freezer burn is easy to recognize: you will see discolored spots, which are almost always white or yellowish white. The presence of frost alone on frozen bait, however, does not indicate freezer burn.

If it happens that you are in an area where dry ice is not available, then use a thick layer of ice (3 to 5 inches) on the bottom of the cooler sprinkled heavily with any kind of salt. Then add bait. Then place a layer of ice and salt on top. It is also a good idea to seal the edges of the cooler with masking tape to keep the air out.

When processing bait, "flash freezing" is the best method; usually, however, only your bait and tackle store or his supplier has the equipment for it. But don't hesitate to use your home freezer; it is perfectly adequate for storing bait, even for months if necessary. When freezing in your home freezer spread your bait out. Don't pile it up and then freeze it. Once it is frozen, then you can pile it up in the freezer.

Refreezing of bait is not recommended unless you are fishing in a place where it is almost impossible to buy, like one of the out islands of the Bahamas where there isn't much else you can do.

When packing bait in plastic bags for freezing make sure you squeeze as much air out of the bag as possible before placing in the freezer. It will help save storage room as well as help protect the bait.

4.

Rigging Basics:
Do's, Don'ts and Knots

There is an old saying that fishing is 90 percent luck. Whether or not this is so is open to question. However, the professional angler makes sure that he keeps as many of the odds as possible in his favor. There are certain general principles which apply to *all* blue water trolling baits. These should become second nature to you.

1. *Always* use a haywire twist for attaching leader wire to hook or making eye for snap swivel.
2. *Always* use a barrel wrap after the haywire twist. This allows you to snap off excess wire and leaves

end smooth without a dangerously sharp burr, which will also snarl in your gloves.

3. Use the 15 feet of leader wire allowed under the International Game Fish rules. Using slightly less is all right, but more will *eliminate* your chances of entering a record fish with the IGFA. When using a line of 80- to 130-pound test you're allowed 30 feet of wire.

4. Coil wire as shown, after making a small eye in one end to slip over snap swivel. Leave 10 to 12 inches of the other end free for rigging.

5. *Always* make sure your leader passes through the eye of the hook.

6. *Always* use either a stainless steel or tinned leader wire. You will lose less fish than with an all-mono leader. Generally, select the smallest diameter wire for your purposes. A heavy #15 wire is fine for giant bluefin tuna but will hamper any swimming qualities you may have had in a small bait.

7. Select the proper size hook for the bait being used.

8. *Always* keep your hooks filed to a razor sharpness. It is even a good idea to file any new hooks you may have bought.

9. Make sure your hook is well centered in any bait you rig. It should neither hang nor bind, and yet still leave enough bite exposed.

10. Always use a very sharp knife with a good blade and point for rigging. While preparing bait keep a whetstone nearby so you can hone your knife every now and then. Cutting bait dulls your knife surprisingly fast.

11. Always make sure the mouth of any bait is closed either by leader wire or stitching.

12. Always wet your gloves before using so they won't slip when wiring a fish.

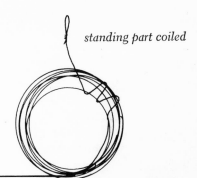

standing part coiled

working end

Rule: Always coil your leaders and leave a working end of 14 to 24 inches. Put a small eye in standing part for snap-swivel.

Rule: Never use barrel wraps alone, but always finish haywire twist with four or five barrel wraps. Haywire twist should look exactly like neck of wire coathanger. Little handle makes it easy to snap off excess wire without leaving dangerous burr.

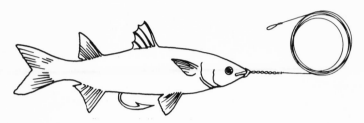

Rule: Coil 15 or 30 feet of leader wire neatly. Using snap-swivel loop, make exactly three under and over wraps to bind coil. Keep coiled leader snug against nose of bait. Above is a rigged bait with leader properly coiled.

Rule: Stitch up belly any way you want to — preferably as above — but make sure you don't stitch too close to hook or it will bind.

half hitch   *clove hitch*   *pipe well hitch*

double clinch knot

finished double clinch knot

improved clinch knot

finished improved clinch knot

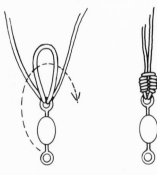

FIG. 1   FIG. 2

Bimini hitch. This knot is used for attaching snap swivel to end of double line. Slip loop through eye of swivel (Figure 1). Next wrap or revolve swivel over loop in middle five or six times. Now maintain pressure on double line and slide knot down to swivel. Knot will finish as in Figure 2.

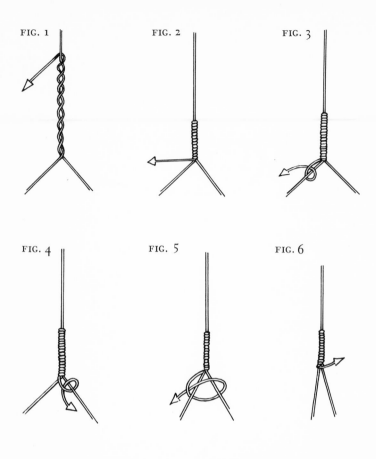

FIG. 1   FIG. 2   FIG. 3

FIG. 4   FIG. 5   FIG. 6

Double line knot (Bimini twist). It takes two people to tie this one. Double your line to 15 to 30 feet (see IGFA rules). Next twist line together for a couple of feet. Now start working end (arrow) down outside of twisted lines. Let your partner grab two legs of loop and separate them. As he does this you pull out and down and your line will roll over and down twisted line (Figure 2). Next, take a half hitch over one leg, then a half hitch over the other leg (Figures 3 and 4). Next take four or five half hitches over both legs (Figure 5), and knot will finish as in Figure 6.

22

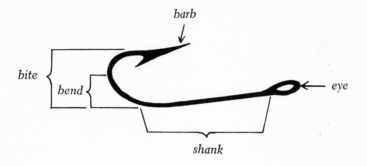

barb

bite

bend

eye

shank

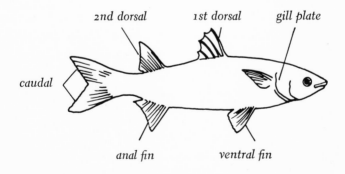

2nd dorsal

1st dorsal

gill plate

caudal

anal fin

ventral fin

23

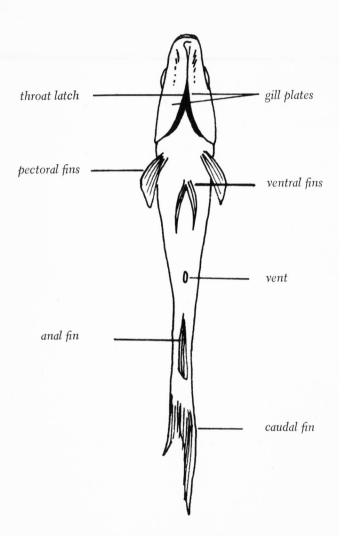

throat latch

gill plates

pectoral fins

ventral fins

vent

anal fin

caudal fin

5.

Basic Baits for the Big Ones

Mullet

Of all the baits discussed, mullet and mackerel are the two best swimming baits. The mullet is relatively flat to begin with (deboning will make him even flatter), and consequently he will swim better when trolled. Of the two varieties, black and silver, the silver is usually preferred because his narrower head allows him to swim better and he has more "flash."

Directions for rigging the basic skipping mullet and

the easiest swimming mullet follow; then on the following pages are fourteen more ways to rig mullet. There are many more ways, but keep in mind that these are basic rigs and apply to bait other than mullet as well. Remember what you have learned while making up basic skipping and swimming baits, then the tricks listed beside each of the remaining twelve will be easy to understand.

If possible, when using processed bait, thaw naturally on ice before rigging. When you catch your own or buy fresh mullet, chill in salt water and ice. When the water has the right amount of ice in it, the mullet will be stiff, but not frozen, within thirty minutes. To prepare freshly caught mullet for your freezer, here's what you do: (1) Chill the bait so it's stiff but not frozen. (2) Cut the bait; that is, debone either with back slit or wedge, gut, and so forth. (3) Brine your bait. (4) Package in plastic bags, squeeze out air and freeze.

To make your brine you need salt, salt or fresh water and ice. Add the salt to the water first. When the water has taken all the salt it can — that is, when you see some has not dissolved — you have added enough. Now you have a freezing brine. The advantage of this method is that you cannot overbrine your bait. Some bait processors use a second brining method. They use a nonfreezing brine and brine overnight. A word of caution on this second method: you have to be very careful about how long you leave the bait in the brine (and this comes only with commercial experience). If you leave it too long in the commercial method, then it can result in overbrining and the bait will not freeze solid when put in the freezer. Both are good, so try them and take your choice as a matter of convenience. Note: Brine must work on the inside of the bait to do any good, which is why you want your bait cut and gutted before putting it in the brine.

Split tail mullet (swimming rig).

For preparation before rigging, all mullet is deboned in one of four ways as shown:

1. *Back Cut.* To start, make a flat cut from just behind the second dorsal coming forward to just behind the head. Next, slit him down the back, removing backbone and guts from top. To remove backbone, start knife blade at rear of head and move back along line made by flat cut; now reverse mullet and do the same on the other side. This is sometimes referred to as the Palm Beach cut.

The Miami cut eliminates the flat cut and leaves both dorsals on the bait. Simply make a slanting cut down and under both dorsals and use fingers to remove backbone.

2. *Deboned Through Gills.* Using a deboner that will fit the size of bait you are working on, lift gill plate and insert deboner upward to front of backbone, then twist deboner as you shove carefully down length of backbone. If you bend fish at end of deboner, then one complete twist of deboner at end will usually free backbone. Next, pull deboner out and backbone will

come with it. Be careful not to cut or break throat latch or come too close to sides near tail. Finally, remove guts by slitting either at vent or behind or between ventral fins. Squeeze guts out. When making this slit keep in mind the size of hook you want to use. Don't make slit so big your hook will hang down.

3. *Wedged and Deboned with Deboner.* Many like this method better than number 2 because there is less chance of damaging the bait when deboning and the end result will swim better. To start, scrape scales off his head with bait knife before making wedge. You should see the soft spot easily at this point. Cut a wedge large enough to admit deboner just behind the eyes. The forward point of the wedge should be just about on his red spot, or maybe a little ahead of it. (Every mullet has a red, gray red, or soft spot on top of his head.) Next, proceed to remove backbone as in number 2 above. Finally, remove guts.

4. *Wedged and Deboned with Knife.* This method allows for the removal of more meat as well as the backbone, and results in an even flatter, better swimming bait. It is good technique when wedging and deboning with a knife to split his tail. This is to facilitate removing his backbone and guts; some believe it gives the bait longer life and better swimming action.

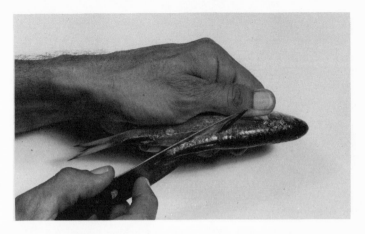

Step 1. Start behind second dorsal fin and make a flat cut forward.

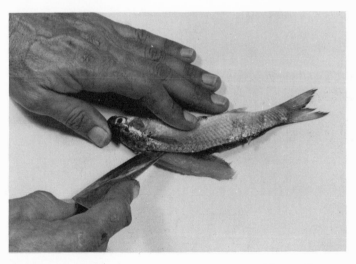

Step 2. Split down back on both sides of backbone. Remove backbone and guts from top.

Step 3. Make small slit for hook just behind ventral fins.

Step 4. Insert hook in slit, pushing it forward until eye is centered under red spot on top of head, or between eyes of mullet.

Step 5. Push leader wire straight down through soft red spot and out lower part of head.

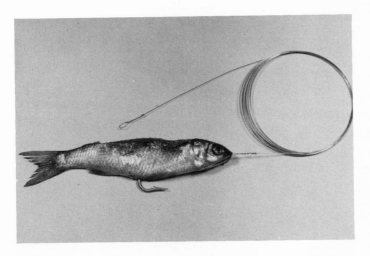

Step 6. Bring end of wire up and over leader, making haywire twist. Finish with barrel wraps and snap off excess. Be sure to start twist next to nose of mullet to keep his mouth closed, or you will have to stitch it shut.

HOW TO RIG THE BASIC SWIMMING MULLET

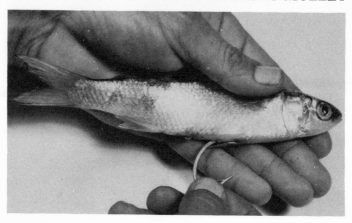

Step 1. Push hook in belly slit and position eye in head. Insert leader wire through head and eye of hook. Now slide lead on working end of leader.

Step 2. Center lead under lower jaw and hold in place while putting haywire twist in wire. Finish with barrel wraps and snap off excess wire. Egg lead should be snug against mouth of mullet to keep it closed.

Step 3. Remember don't overlead your bait. A half-ounce egg lead should be good for mullet up to 7 or 8 inches. Faster trolling speeds or choppy water might require more lead, as will big marlin or tuna baits.

DEBONING MULLET THROUGH GILLS

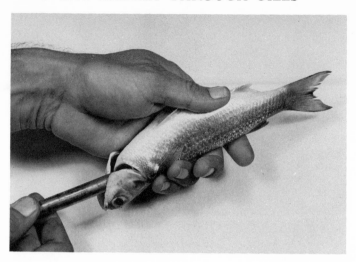

Step 1. Use proper size deboner to fit bait. Lift gill plate and insert deboner upward to front of backbone.

Step 2. Twist deboner as you shove it carefully down length of backbone. Bend tail of mullet and give one complete twist to free backbone.

Step 3. Remove deboner and backbone will come with it. Use wooden push rod to clear deboner. Finally, make slit at vent and squeeze out guts.

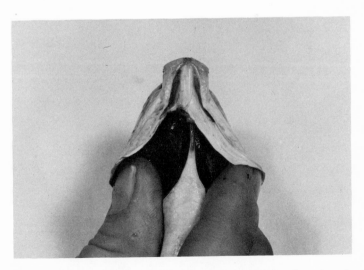

Note: Take care not to break or cut throat latch when inserting deboner.

35

DEBONING MULLET THROUGH WEDGE

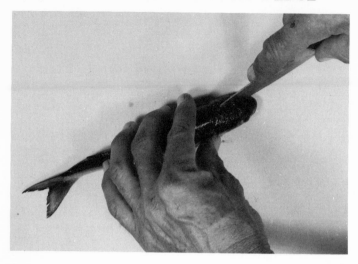

Step 1. Insert knife behind head and cut through skull to about red spot.

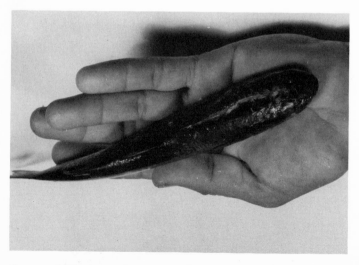

Step 2. Make second cut on other side of head and remove wedge. Opening should appear as in illustration.

Step 3. Twist deboner as you shove it carefully down length of backbone. Bend tail of mullet; give one complete twist to free backbone. Make cut at vent and squeeze to remove guts.

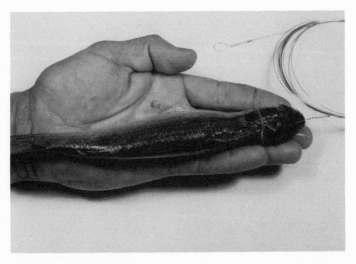

Step 4. Tie head tightly with linen thread to flatten and close forward part of wedge.

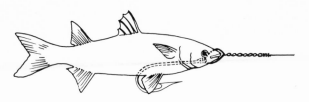

1. Skipping bait. Slit back and remove backbone. Use tight loop to close mouth. Mouth tears easily if open when trolled. Make slit between ventral fins for hook.

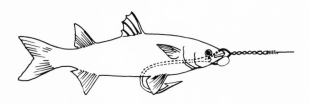

2. Swimming bait. Same as above but swims instead of skips. Put lead on leader after inserting wire through head and eye of hook.

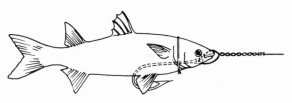

3. Same as 1 but deboned through gill slit. Tie head tightly with linen thread to flatten. This rig is a shortcut to wedging and deboning.

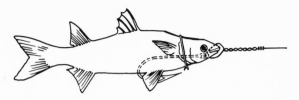

4. Same as 3 but wedged and deboned. Swims better and slightly deeper than 3, and will troll longer.

5. A double hooked 1. Open eye of second hook, slip over barb of first and close. Or use needle eye, slipping shank through ring eye of second hook. Don't make slit for hook as 1, but lay hooks in back slit. Position eye of first hook between eyes of mullet, then push barb through belly. Bring second hook back, but not too far to avoid binding; push through.

6. Deboned through gills and double hooked. Use belly slit for hook. Insert second hook first, pushing barb and bite out vent. Take first hook up through eye of second and work forward to head position. If hook binds, make small slit in vent.

7. Wedged, deboned and double hooked. Same as 6 but swims better.

8. Prerigged hook inserted through and under gill plate. Rig used when bait is chopped off behind hook. Allows putting hook as far back as necessary. Same as mackerel rig (see page 51). If slit is wrong and hook hangs down loosely, take a single support stitch through bait and directly under shank of hook.

9. Same as 8 but wedged and deboned. Mash head and tie off with linen thread.

10. Head rig. Middle about 24 inches of linen thread. Make clove hitch and slip over hook. Let thread hang down on each side for sewing. Stitch hook tightly to head above eyes. Stitch mouth closed. Take a single stitch through gill plates and through body. Tie off with knot.

11. Identical to 10, but hook stitched tightly to nose of bait.

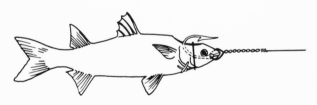

12. Head rig. Cut wedge in top of head. Insert hook with bite coming out forward edge of wedge hole. Next, insert leader wire through head and eye of hook. Wedge hole is closed by tying flat with linen thread. Eliminates need for stitching and sewing.

41

13. Double hooked head rig. Use cable and sleeve to attach second hook. Pass cable through eye of first hook and crimp. Repeat with second hook. Allow enough cable to position second hook first. Wedge and debone bait. Sew first hook on head. Make belly slit, then insert second hook under gill plate and out slit.

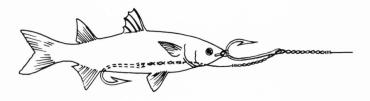

14. Same as 13 but a little neater job. On both rigs second hook is inserted under gill plate cover.

Ballyhoo (Balao)

Ballyhoo is almost always rigged as a skipping bait, although when schooling fish such as dolphin are thick, it is often just slapped on a hook and thrown overboard. It is not only an excellent small bait, but in the giant (12 to 14 inches) or "horse" size makes an excellent blue marlin bait. Ballyhoo does not need slitting, cutting or gutting. However, if he seems fat to you, then use thumb and forefinger to strip gut back and out of his vent. Fresh ballyhoo is preferred over frozen if available and in good condition.

Your ballyhoo rig is made up outside of the bait, and can often be used over and over again.

To start, measure your hook and approximate length of haywire twist you are going to need, as illustrated. If you have any doubt about the appearance of a good haywire twist, then just look at the neck of any wire coathanger. Your hook is going to be positioned so the barb comes out just aft of the ventral fins, and the spur so that it is positioned just forward of the eyes. This is what you measure: the distance between hook position and spur position.

Now put the end of the leader wire through the eye of the hook, bend in loop and lay over leader. At the crossing point hold firmly with either pliers or fingers, then twist both wires together using thumb and index finger of other hand. Barrel wrap the end left from haywire twist around leader at right angles as shown. Leave a spur of from ¼ to ¾ inch sticking straight up. The length of the spur depends on the size of the ballyhoo.

Now hold the ballyhoo so that his back is curved in the palm of your hand. This is a big help in getting the

43

hook back where you want it without damaging the bait. Next, open gill plate cover with point of hook and insert hook with leader attached. Guide hook gently back, letting the bend in the hook follow the bend in the bait. When you have worked the hook back until the spur on the front of the rig is just in front of his eyes, push the barb of the hook through his belly, keeping barb and belly well centered. Now pull back gently on hook and, as you do, place exposed haywire twist under gill plate and along throat latch. Take the spur next and push it up through both jaws and out top of head.

There are many ways of using the copper wire in the final step, but only two are worth consideration. The first one is: wrap copper wire once behind spur and then through eyes. Pull wire snug and wrap once more behind spur. Now wrap wire down bill until wire runs out. Finish by snapping off remaining portion of bill with fingers. This method both secures the head firmly to the hook and saves you the trouble of plucking his eyes out. With other ballyhoo rigs the eyes are going to have to come out. If you neglect this, the eyes will bug out after being trolled and ruin the action of the bait.

The second method requires one wrap behind and under the gill plate. Then pull snug and wrap behind spur and down bill; finish off as above. Some say this rig keeps his head on the hook better, but you are going to have to pluck his eyes out before using. Either rig is good, so choose the one that's easiest for you.

Occasionally, for the sake of variety, ballyhoo are rigged with a brightly colored plastic skirt, which is simply slipped on leader wire and allowed to slide down to his nose when trolled. It is not a bad idea and won't hurt the action.

One Last Rig

An exceptional bait for kingfish is to cut a ballyhoo the same as the basic rig for a swimming mullet — no spur and no copper wire. Double hook and troll very slowly.

HOW TO RIG BALLYHOO

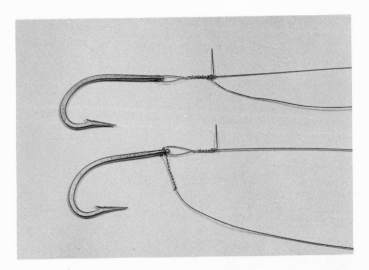

Step 1. Make up ballyhoo rigs outside of bait. Top rig is for wrapping copper wire through eyes. Bottom rig for wrapping copper wire behind gills. Either one is good.

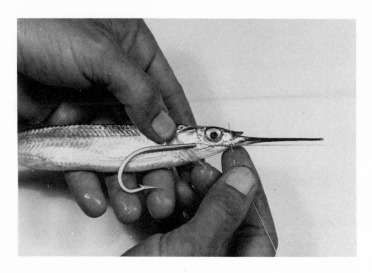

Step 2. Measure your hook for approximate length of haywire twist you are going to need.

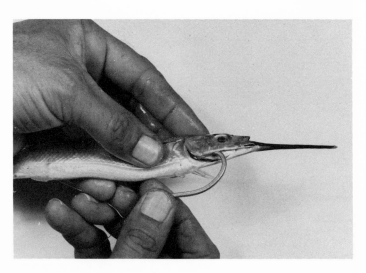

Step 3. Open gill plate cover with point of hook, and insert hook with leader attached.

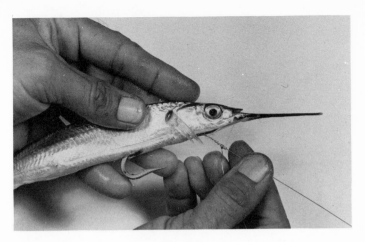

Step 4. Work hook back until spur on front is just ahead of his eyes. Push barb of hook through belly.

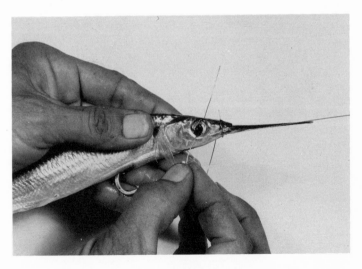

Step 5. Pull back gently on hook; as you do, place exposed hay-wire twist under gill plate. Take spur next and push up through jaws and out top of head. To finish, wrap copper wire once behind spur and then through eyes. Pull wire snug and wrap once more behind spur. Now wrap wire down bill until wire runs out. Snap off remaining portion of bill with fingers.

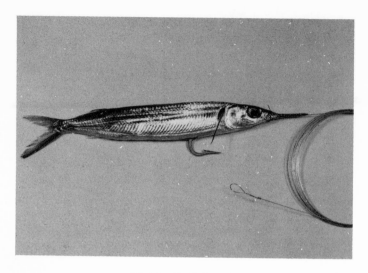

Finished ballyhoo rig.

Variation with plastic skirt.

Mackerel

Mackerel, along with mullet, is the other excellent swimming bait in common use. It is very tough, and a good one can be trolled all day long. When using mackerel, the angler is almost always going after marlin or tuna. Bait stores generally carry them from ½ to 3 pounds; preferred size is ¼ to 1¼ pounds. When buying mackerel, be sure his yellow spots are still fairly bright and that he was gutted before freezing. And don't accept bait with cloudy or sunken eyes unless you must. The same is true of freezer-burned bait. This applies to all bait.

There are at least a half-dozen mackerel rigs and even variations of these; many seem to be nothing more than whims of the angler. However there are two basic mackerel rigs the professional big game fisherman needs to learn: the belly rig and the head rig. Head rigs are sometimes identified as Australian or New Zealand rigs, which makes no difference at all in rigging or catching fish!

1. You start by rigging your hook out of the fish, the same as ballyhoo, but leave a longer spur (4") because of the bigger bait.
2. Insert rig up to spur through gill opening and out slit in belly where he has been gutted.
3. Next, bring spur up through lower and upper jaws forward of the eyes at about the point you see his nostril vents.
4. Now bring the spur over his nose and take three barrel wraps — you don't need any more. With the remainder of wire bend at right angle and snap off by twisting back and forth parallel to leader.
5. Then pull back gently on exposed part of hook to

make sure that leader and eye of hook are lying straight inside of bait.

6. To complete bait sew up belly. With 24 to 30 inches of linen thread to work with, insert needle first through gills, then cross-stitch down to vent and back up to gills, making an "X" and bypassing the hook as illustrated. The hook will bind if your stitching goes right up to the bite. Keep your stitching in lower (toughest) part of belly, or about ⅜ inch up the sides. Too far up hits the soft part of the fish and is likely to tear under stress of trolling.

7. A lot of experienced anglers will say the spur wire alone is enough to keep his mouth closed. Professionals, however, usually take a single stitch to either side of leader wire, through upper and lower jaws, tying off remaining thread with a knot.

Errors to Watch For

Remember, if you overhook (use one too big), your bait will lose some action; underhooking does not leave enough bite showing. Also, if your hook is too far back it ruins the swimming action. On the belly rig, if the hook is too far forward you will miss strikes. Keep your hook back about one third of the distance between the ventral fins and the vent.

Note: With a little practice you should be able to belly rig a mackerel in 2 to 5 minutes or less and troll him all day long.

For giant bluefin tuna add a lead under his chin to make him swim. All tuna bait swims perfectly upright, not over on the side or with any slow rolls. Don't prerig as above, but insert hook and rig as you would in the basic swimming mullet.

Head Rig

As long as the hook is firmly stitched to the head, and mouth, gills and belly are sewn closed, you're in business. Put a clove hitch on shank just before bite of hook, and let the ends of thread hang down as illustrated. This is a skipping bait and identical to the head rig used on mullet.

HOW TO RIG MACKEREL

Step 1. Make rig the same as you would for ballyhoo but leave a longer spur, about 4 inches. Insert rig through gill opening and out slit in belly.

Step 2. Bring spur up through jaws and out top of head. Now bring spur over nose and take three barrel wraps around leader wire. Snap off excess wire.

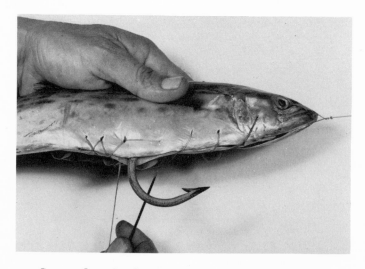

Step 3. Complete bait by sewing up belly as illustrated.

Finished mackerel bait.

Strip Bait

Strip bait is often thought of as a substitute for the more sophisticated mullet and mackerel rigs. It is not. It is a deadly swimming or skipping bait with distinct advantages for the angler. Strip bait is the fastest and easiest of all baits to rig. Most of the time it is available at your local bait and tackle shop, or it can be cut from almost any fish caught.

When you are going to cut strips, if at all possible use the common bonito (false albacore). If you cannot get bonito, then cut strips from mackerel, kingfish or dolphin belly, or fillet a mullet. When using a mullet fillet as a strip, leave the scales on to prevent curling

53

while being trolled. For more trolling action with a mullet strip, split his tail as you fillet.

Unless desperate for bait, don't cut your strips from the flanks or upper portions of the fish; these are the softer parts and don't wear well at all. Note: While pork rind has its place on board your boat, it is no substitute for strips made from real fish.

Strip baits have a real advantage because they are relatively weedless, and therefore ideal if you are after dolphin in heavily scattered weed patches. And don't overlook or forget the fact that a good strip can catch anything that swims, and has!

Cutting Strips

With the point of your knife cut through skin to general shape and length of bait desired as shown. The length of your strip can be anywhere from 1½ inches for school dolphin to 10 inches or more for blue or white marlin. After you have made your cut, lift one end with fingers, pull up a little, slide knife under strip and slice away from fish.

Next, plane or shave the meat side to anywhere from ⅛ to ¼ inch thick. Feather your strip at a 45-degree angle along the edges. Point the tail and square the head.

Note: The meat of whatever fish you use has a grain; when fishing, always troll your bait with the grain. Trolling against the grain will pull the meat loose, or ruffle it and spoil the action. Keep the grain in mind when determining which end you are going to use for the head of the bait.

To keep strips fresh, salt meat side lightly and put directly on ice or on top of damp newspaper in cooler. For storing, salt, put in plastic bags and freeze.

There are three basic strip rigs:

1. A haywire twist rig.
2. A safety pin rig.
3. A fixed safety pin rig.

Haywire Twist Rig

Holding the strip in your hand lay the hook down the center so the eye is well within the flat or rounded end, then push the barb of the hook through the bait. Insert leader wire through bait and eye of hook and finish with haywire twist and barrel wrap.

Safety Pin Rig

This rig allows you to place the hook in the bait anyplace along the center line. This is particularly effective when kingfish are cutting off your strips short of the hook.

Make this rig exactly as you would a ballyhoo rig, but leave a longer spur (about 3 inches), and make a safety pin clip as illustrated.

Fixed Safety Pin Rig

For a fixed safety pin rig wrap leader wire behind and through eye of hook before making haywire twist and safety pin clip.

The advantage of this rig is that when the hook is placed well back in the bait it keeps the wrap through the eye from rolling on the hook.

When rigging for strips push your hook through the meat side first. The only reason for this is that it's easier and therefore more efficient. We have never been able to verify whether a strip bait is more effective trolled skin side up or skin side down.

Here again, to make a swimming bait and add variety, place a trolling feather or plastic skirt in front of the bait by simply sliding it on your leader before rigging. It will stay on ahead of the bait when trolled, so don't worry about trying to fasten it to the leader.

HOW TO RIG STRIP BAIT

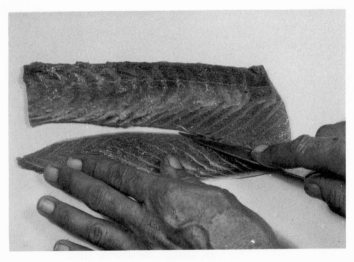

Step 1. With point of knife cut through skin to general shape and length of bait desired as shown.

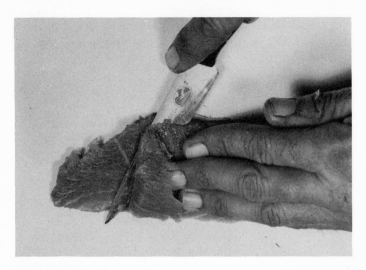

Step 2. Next, plane or shave the meat side to anywhere from ⅛ to ¼ inch thick.

Step 3. Point the tail and square the head. Keep the grain with the head. Going against the grain will pull the meat loose and spoil the action when trolled. For more action, split tail of strip behind hook.

Step 4. Two rigs are illustrated. For a safety pin rig, make it exactly as you would a ballyhoo rig, but leave a longer spur (about 3 inches) and bend a safety pin clip as illustrated. For a fixed safety pin rig, wrap wire behind and through eye of hook before making haywire twist and safety pin clip.

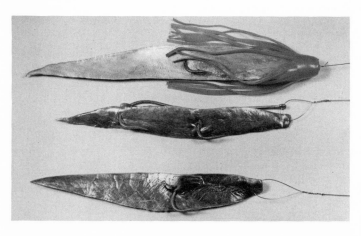

Two finished strip baits using third rig, which is simply a loop through the bait and eye of hook finished off with haywire twist and barrel wraps. Top rig shows placement of plastic skirt for variety.

Squid Rigs

Any discussion of how to rig a squid must take into consideration his strange body: not being a fish, he has no backbone. A squid is in fact a cephalopod, whose name is a combination of two Greek words meaning "head and foot." His tentacles (10 of them) surround and are a part of his head. He swims just as fast backward as forward, but is trolled by his tail or caudal fin.

A good squid has a fresh white pink or cream pink color and when bad turns brick red, or even purple. Fresh water should *never* come in contact with squid, much less be used for thawing. For keeping squid fresh on board, place in shallow pan on top of ice in cooler. When freezing, separate in plastic bags or wrap carefully in aluminum foil. There is no need to brine it.

No cutting is necessary to rig squid, although there is a kind of gutting process. Whether you are rigging a small 4- or 5-ounce squid or a large one over a pound, hold him by the tail and with your other hand squeeze gently, but firmly, down the length of his mantle — more like milking than gutting. The milk coming out the open end of the body near his head is his guts.

Almost all squid are made up as skipping baits. There are two simple ways to rig a squid; the dozens of others known are complicated variations that have the same end result as these two. All squid rigs require that you sew or hitch his head to his body. Like all other baits, make sure he is rigged evenly down the center line.

Rig with Lead

To repeat, you are going to secure the head to the body. This rig is made up outside of the squid, and has to be measured carefully. Measure from the very end or point of the tail to about ½ inch from the end of the mantle. This is because once you've inserted the hook in his head, you are going to pull his head into his body about this distance. See illustrations A and B. Notice the head is pulled back up to dotted line, Figure A, and positioned as in Figure B.

Figure C illustrates the prerigging of the bait after measuring. Simply make your haywire twist to secure hook, then take three or four barrel wraps; now take some "lazy" turns up to sinker position and finish with barrel wraps. In this way neither the sinker nor the squid can slide down leader to hook.

Figure D shows hook imbedded in head of squid between eyes. Before you put the hook in the head, however, insert leader in body and out through point in tail. Because his body is soft you can feel and guide leader to tail point with your fingers.

Now insert your hook in his head between his eyes and pull leader until lead is snug in tail position. The only thing that remains to do is to take a few stitches with bait needle and linen thread. Take a stitch to fasten head to body and another one through body and around leader wire.

Double Hook Squid Rig

This is the same as the single hook rig described above, but add a second hook as shown in Figure F. Measure for hook to be inserted in head first, then forward for second hook. Place the second hook anyplace you want from the middle of the body forward. The bite of the aft hook will be down, the bite of the forward hook up.

HOW TO RIG SQUID

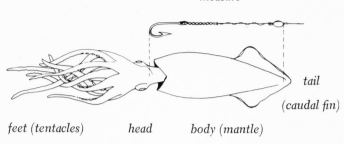

measure

tail

(caudal fin)

feet (tentacles)   *head*   *body (mantle)*

Squid rig using lead as stopper to keep body from sliding down to hook when trolled.

FIG. A

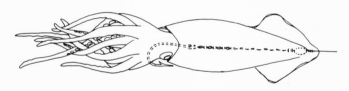

Rig inserted in squid before stitching. Lead is pulled snug to point in caudal fin, and hook is inserted in meaty part of head between eyes.

FIG. B

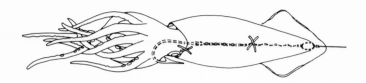

Use a single stitch to secure head to body. Take another stitch
through body and around leader and tie off tightly.

FIG. C

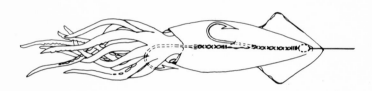

Double hooked squid rig with bite of head hook down and body
hook up.

FIG. D

Step 1. For either a single or double hook lead, rig measured length between lead and hook against side of squid.

Step 2. Insert rig in mantle and pull forward until lead is snug in point of caudal fin.

63

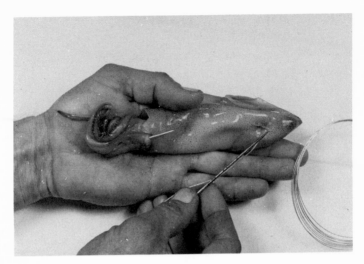

Step 3. Take a single stitch to secure head to body or mantle. Then take another stitch through body and around leader wire. Pull tight and tie off with a knot.

Finished squid rig.

Eels

Eels are perhaps the toughest of all natural baits. You can troll them all day long, or for three or four days, and sometimes two or three fish may be taken on the same bait. This is one reason bait and tackle stores quite often carry them prerigged.

On the northeastern coast of the United States, where eels are caught for both food and bait purposes, they are generally available fresh in stores; in the South you can buy them heavily brined or fresh in retail fish markets.

Eel has excellent freezing qualities, and you can keep them frozen for months with good results.

The eels you rig will be anywhere from a foot long to more than 2 feet long for blue marlin.

You do not need to cut, gut or really even measure to rig an eel. If he appears fat in the belly, then hold on as best you can — "slippery as an eel" is a fact — and squeeze, sliding your hand down to the vent to empty him.

Basic Eel Rig

Secure hook to leader with haywire twist and barrel wraps and snap off excess (Figure A). Insert leader in vent and out mouth (Figure B). Leave enough bite on hook showing. Next, twist black swivel on wire at eel's mouth. Finish with stitch to close mouth and gills. It is very important when taking this stitch to go through swivel and tie off with knot. This is to keep him from sliding down wire to hook when trolled.

As with other baits, if hook binds at all, free it by making small slit at front of vent.

HOW TO RIG EELS

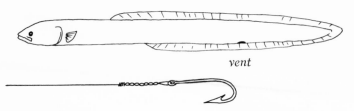

vent

Secure hook with haywire twist and barrel wraps. Snap off excess.

FIG. A

Insert leader through vent and out mouth. Leave enough bite showing. Secure forward end of leader to swivel for sewing purposes.

FIG. B

Stitch gills and mouth closed. Sew head to leader by finishing stitches through eye of swivel. Tie off.

FIG. C

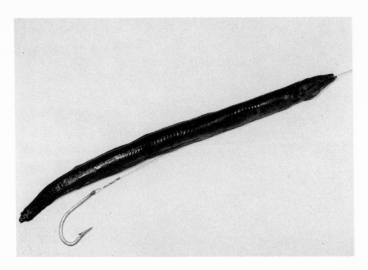

Step 1. Insert wire with hook in vent and out through mouth.

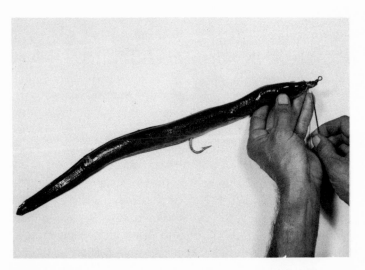

Step 2. Secure wire to swivel at mouth and stitch gills and mouth closed. Attach bait to leader by finishing stitches through swivel. Tie off.

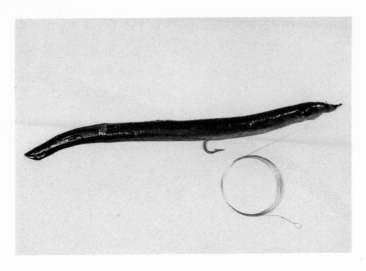

Finished eel rig.

Bonefish, Ladyfish and Bonito

These baits are generally used for blue marlin because they are large baits, sometimes reaching 4 or 5 pounds. They are almost always rigged as skipping baits, or, as these big baits are called, "splashers."

Once you've rigged one or two splashers, it's easy: no deboning, no gutting; sew hook to head, stitch mouth closed. Next, take a single stitch through gill plates and lower part of body, tie off and you're done!

For storing, chill in ice and sea water, then freeze. Brining is not required, but if you prefer, then go ahead and brine and freeze. Either method is good. Remember, you can also use a belly rig, but a head rig is easier and works as well.

While all of these fish call for the same head or belly rigs, here are a few things to remember:

1. Bonefish. It is illegal to buy or sell bonefish in Florida. Freezing bonefish is not a good idea. Freezing will cut the trolling life of bonefish in half, particularly small ones. Get fresh bonefish if possible; when they are not available and you must use frozen ones, remember to change them frequently because they wash out quickly.

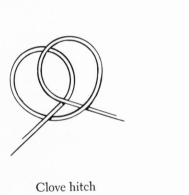

Clove hitch

Clove hitch over bend of hook with ends long enough for stitching.

2. Ladyfish. Although seasonal, they can be bought at many bait and tackle stores. Unlike bonefish, they freeze well. While many people brine ladyfish before freezing, it is not recommended here; brining takes some of the silver out and tends to yellow the bait.

3. Ladyfish have hard, sharp edges on their jaws. Keep all stitching away from these edges.
4. Handle all scale fish with care. The more scales left on, the better, because they preserve the flashing and lasting qualities of the bait. Scales are tough and protect the bait against wear when trolled.
5. Bonito. They are almost never available in bait stores. Freezing results are very, very poor, so bonito are used almost exclusively by being caught on a house line while trolling for other gamefish.
6. For small bonito — 14 inches or under — use a belly rig for better hooking qualities. Belly rig the same as you would with bonefish or ladyfish.

Belly rig (same idea as basic ballyhoo rig).

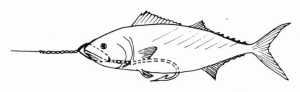

Bonito, belly rigged.

Ladyfish, belly rigged.

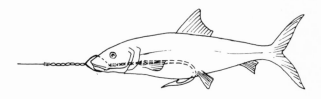

Bonefish, belly rigged.

Two More Rigs Worth Trying

Here are two more rigs that almost span the history of blue water trolling baits. One of them, the Palm Beach rig, is old and seldom seen anymore; the other, known as a daisy chain, is relatively new. Both are unusual, both expand your bag of tricks for luring the big ones to your hook.

The Palm Beach rig is very effective; the daisy chain can be deadly on all billfish and tuna at times.

The Palm Beach or Throat Latch Rig

Starting at front end of second dorsal, make diagonal cut forward to front end of throat latch. Be careful not to damage throat latch because this is very important to the bait's action. Discard head, gills and top half of mullet. Next, remove backbone, guts and some meat. Position hook with barb up and lay in bait. Now secure leader wire, but make haywire twist long enough to extend beyond front end of throat latch.

Stitch forward end of bait closed and secure throat latch by half hitching, or with a pipe well hitch, to leader. Finish by placing clove hitch over bait and hook as shown. This will close body cavity and anchor hook.

Although this bait takes more time to rig, it will swim better than any other in your arsenal.

Daisy Chain Rig

This one takes about four times as long to rig as a single troller, but then you don't get to drag a whole "school" of bait without a little effort. The daisy chain is especially popular in "P" town and Barnstable, Massachusetts, for bluefin tuna; it is an excellent rig for billfish as well. The daisy chain can be rigged from mullet, squid or ballyhoo. In each case the only difference in bait preparation is that the last one in the chain will have a hook in it and the others (up to seven) will not. In other words, rig the baits so they will last as long as the last one, i.e., debone or sew according to the type of bait used on the "chain."

Step 1. Starting at front end of second dorsal, make diagonal cut forward to front end of throat latch. Do not damage throat latch. Discard head, gills and top half of mullet.

Step 2. Next, remove backbone and some meat as illustrated.

73

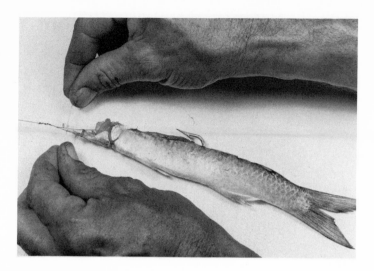

Step 3. Position hook with barb up where you want it. Next, secure leader wire but make haywire twist long enough to extend beyond front end of throat latch.

Step 4. Now stitch forward end of bait closed and secure by half hitches, or pipe well hitch, to leader.

74

Step 5. To finish, place clove hitch over bait and hook as shown. This will anchor hook and close body cavity.

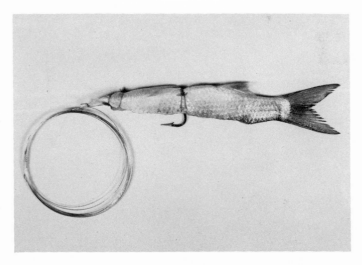

Finished bait.

DAISY CHAIN RIG

Rig just as you would if trolling singly, but put hook only in last bait. Use at least four baits on daisy chain. On all baits, except the one with a hook, half hitch or use pipe well hitch to attach each bait to leader.

6.

Other Baits, or What to Do When Your Bait Box Is Empty

No one has ever proved that fish forget things, but not so with anglers. The suggestions in this section are designed to stop the symptoms of forgetfulness, that is, cussing the fish and threats to sell the boat. So when you have forgotten to take enough bait with you, or have just plain forgotten to take bait, here are some of the things you can do.

Let's say, for example, that you are out of bait — perhaps the kingfish have eaten up the two dozen ballyhoo you brought along. No need to go home. Just start trolling a 3½ Drone or Reflecto spoon, or feathers. It is not

77

guaranteed, but chances are usually good for you to pick up some bonito or dolphin. As soon as you do, simply make strips or live bait, depending on the size of fish caught, and you're back in business!

If you run into "grasshoppers" (small school dolphin), then remember to leave one overboard until the next one is hooked, then bring in the first one and leave the second in the water, etc. In this way you will keep the school with you for a surprisingly long time.

And while we're on dolphin we should mention flying fish! Very often, if you gut a dolphin right away, you'll find a flying fish he's inhaled that's still in good enough shape for rigging. Rig the flying fish the same as you would a ballyhoo or one of the basic mullet rigs. Depending on the size of the flying fish, insert hook into vent, or forward of it. Punch leader wire through both jaws and eye of hook, then make your haywire twist and barrel wraps to finish.

If the flying fish is large, then rig as you would a mackerel. Make a long wrap from eye of hook up leader and leave a 3-inch spur. Make a belly slit and gut. Insert rig through gill covering and bring bite of hook out belly slit. Finish by inserting spur through both jaws and out top of head; bring end of spur over nose, take three barrel wraps around leader and you're done. (If necessary, stitch belly closed.)

You might find that you like flying fish for variety. If so, quite a few bait and tackle shops carry them. They freeze well or can be used fresh. At night they are attracted to light like a moth, and often will "fly" into your cockpit. Anyway you get them, they make good bait.

In the last few years there have been more and more boats going farther and farther in their quest for big gamefish. This is particularly true of boats going to the Bahama Islands off of Florida's eastern coast. Generally these boats are hunting marlin and are gone for two, three or four days, sometimes a couple of weeks. The amount of bait to carry on this kind of trip is often difficult to judge, and is impossible to buy in some areas of the islands. And it is *very* expensive to fly in. Here are some effective alternatives to those baits already mentioned: cero mackerel, rainbow runners, barracuda, and dolphin. All make excellent substitute baits for marlin fishing. Just use any of the head rigs or swimming rigs described under mullet, mackerel, bonefish, ladyfish and bonito.

One thing to remember: carry a variety of feathers and spoons. Vary the sizes of spoons and sizes and colors in feathers. When color is mentioned we don't want to start an argument about whether fish can see actual colors or distinguish between light waves and intensities. The only thing you will discover is that color doesn't seem to make a great deal of difference trolling, but bottom fishing and deep trolling are a little different. For example, grouper will hit feathers, so if you want to be sure of a good fish dinner and you are out of bait, then try a red and black or a yellow feather. If you want kingfish for dinner and you are out of bait, then double hook a feather for them. Use a white, red and white or a yellow one.

Not long ago a good angler and his family went fun fishing for a half a day. The children were small so it was more of a boat ride. When they started trolling they had only a few feathers and a couple of spoons. Right off they caught a bonito and a little blackfin tuna. Using these to make strips, they ended their day with a kingfish and two sailfish!

So if you run out of bait, or forget it, don't give up. Just open your tackle box for spoons and feathers, then make strips from what you catch. Or use what you catch for live bait, or rig whole for marlin.

79

7.

Live Bait

Almost anything that swims is potential live bait. Three species, however, are preferred: (1) blue runners, (2) goggle eyes, and (3) bonito (false albacore). These three are preferred south of Oregon Inlet, Cape Hatteras, North Carolina; north of there, Atlantic mackerel and even live squid have been used by Captain Larry Hastings with good results. Small dolphin are good anyplace in the world. Because live bait is very hard to buy, you will, in all likelihood, be catching your own.

Live bait is always a good producer wherever you find

blue water. In many areas at certain times of the year, it is easily the best bait to use. One disadvantage of live baiting is that you must troll very slowly and you don't cover much water. This is particularly true in marlin fishing, where you want to cover as much territory as possible.

Catching Your Own Live Bait

For blue runners troll very close to shore, near inshore reefs and over rocky bottom. Use one to four yellow or white mackerel feathers tied to 12- to 20-pound test monofilament line — you don't want it any heavier. Use about a 4-inch mono leader going to line and space feathers 8 to 12 inches apart (Figure C). If they're proving hard to catch try a wire (monel) line to a cigar-shaped lead, then a 20-foot, 20-pound mono leader tied to a oo or ooo Drone or Reflecto spoon. Let lead bump on bottom; be careful when near rocks. Jig feathers when trolling. Spoon does not have to be jigged.

Bonito are caught offshore or inshore using a single feather or spoon. If you have a choice, you'll probably do somewhat better with a feather trolled 15 to 40 feet back of the boat. You do not need to jig for bonito although it helps, especially if you are missing strikes. Bonito is the preferred live bait for any big game fish. Why? Experience is the only reason we can give.

Goggle eyes are caught the same as blue runners, but troll shorter and slower and jig faster. They're harder to catch than "runners," but the game fish seem to like them better. At the same time, they don't last as well in captivity nor are they as hardy when trolled — so take your choice!

Here are some general comments on live baiting worth remembering:

The trolling speed for live baiting is very slow — a little faster than a drift — to keep the bait alive.

Best results are obtained when a lead is not used on your leader wire.

Live bait really doesn't keep well more than 24 hours. The bait gets bumped, skinned up and plain tired in captivity. It is a good idea to try and catch new live bait every day; it's much better than using live bait kept overnight. And bonito *won't* live in a live well at all.

When using bonito, handle as little as possible. They die easily out of water, but once returned, they're as hardy as ever.

Once live bait has been hit and cut, and even though still alive, change your bait immediately.

When live baiting it is always a good idea to offset the bite of the hook by bending with a pair of pliers.

If fishing is red hot and you are sewing your bait on, then it's a good idea to have a couple of live baits rigged in the well minus the leader wire.

Remember, when using more than one hook, measure where you are going to insert the second hook, so that as the bait is trolled the hooks don't stand up, but lie parallel to the bait.

Rig for sewing on live bait through eyes.

Figure A. Simplest single hook rig. Just make sure you insert hook ahead of dorsal fin, as close to head and as deep as possible without hitting the backbone.

Figure B. Double hook rig. Insert barb of second hook just under skin on side of fish.

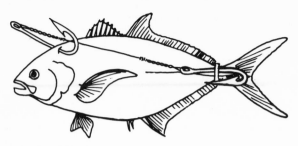

Figure C. Double hook rig. Second hook secured to side by rubber band around tail.

Figure D. Double hook rig. Measure so shanks of hooks parallel bait as shown.

Figure E. Triple hook rig. Three hooks connected by swivels: two in bait, one hanging.

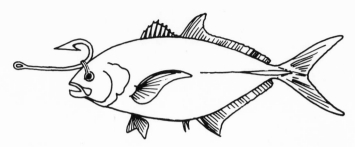

Figure F. Eye rig. At the top of a fish's eye socket is a soft spot; some call it the hole. When you insert a bait needle here it will go straight through and come out the top of the other eye socket with little damage to the bait. Start with linen thread and a clove hitch over shank of hook as with other head rigs. Insert needle through "hole" at top of the eye, pull hook snug to head and tie off. This rig is often used because it is harder for a fish to steal your bait. It will swim a little shallower than other baits, but don't worry about it. If you're going to use this rig on bonito then have a few made up and ready to go. Remember, you want a bonito back in the water as fast as possible so he doesn't die.

Figure G. "Ha-ha" rig. Striking fish, especially kingfish, often attack the bait from the side or head and cut or cut off your bait. Put bait on either top or bottom hook. The free dangling hook will often catch a fish you would have otherwise missed by snagging him, thus it's "ha-ha, I fooled you!"

8.

Matching the Bait and the Fish

Blue Marlin

There are probably more anglers who would rather catch a blue marlin than any other species in the ocean. This is because his size, speed, bad temper and rarity make him about the toughest challenge in big game sportfishing. What follows are a few tips and some experience that will definitely increase your chances to boat a blue.

Although rare when compared to most other game

fish, literally thousands have been caught over the years. His huge appetite and sheer bulk make him one of the biggest hogs in the ocean. When he is hungry he will even gulp down small sailfish to fill his stomach. As for size of bait, the analysis of the stomach contents of blue marlin shows they have eaten dolphin topping 30 pounds.

On the other hand, he can frustrate the devil out of any angler when he's "window-shopping" the baits. But when he's going to eat he usually colors up, lights up like a neon sign just before the attack.

When it comes to how he eats, many believe that he always uses his bill to kill bait. *Not so!* Sometimes he might slash at the bait, but in most cases he comes in with his mouth wide open. His bill is a tool used both as an offensive and defensive mechanism. For example, one boat captain while fishing off of Bimini saw (with witnesses) a blue marlin beating a shark with his bill on the surface. After the marlin killed the shark, the angler hooked and boated the fish! And there are many cases where a piece of a marlin's bill has been found broken off and imbedded in fish, including other marlin. In other instances he uses his bill to probe the sea bottom for food, as proved by his stomach containing the remains of the bottom-feeding grouper.

To rig up for blue marlin, select a bait from ¼ to 3 pounds, preferably ½ to 1½ pounds. Use a large hook; Soby, Martu, Sea Demon, or Seamate are recommended. Choose a belly rigged mackerel or mullet for bait. And, as with all billfish, vary the menu by using both swimmers and splashers.

Because a blue marlin is a scarce fish, you want to hunt him over as large an area as possible while trolling. Blues are usually found alone, although not infrequently they

Blue marlin.

travel in pairs and on occasions in bunches. This means that if you do hook one, it's a good idea to stay in the same area and look for a companion fish. Now and again you will see one swimming lazily along the surface, "tailing." When this is the case he usually doesn't want to eat, but you never know, so present your bait in front of him anyway.

As you would for most other blue water fish, try dragging your baits where you see indications of weed lines,

An excellent blue marlin bait: belly rigged mackerel.

color changes in the water ("the rip"), birds working over bait concentrations, etc. And still, about half the time, you'll find blue marlin anyplace in the open ocean with no indications present.

As a general rule your best chances will come from trolling along a sharp dropoff. Marlin fishing depth in Florida and the Bahamas, for example, will be the hundred-fathom curve to the big depths 3 to 10 miles offshore. In the Atlantic the westerly edge of the Gulf Stream curves east as it moves north. This means that as you move north you are going to have to hunt blues farther from shore. For instance, off southern Florida you can troll for them within a mile or two of shore, off of Ocean City miles from shore, and in Montauk, Long Island, up to 60 or more miles.

There are all kinds of stories about how a marlin will take your bait head first or tail first. The fact is he will attack your bait from the head, tail, side — anywhere!

The important thing to remember when he strikes is to drop back on him. A rule of thumb is that when you "feel" the fish, put the reel in gear and try him. The drop back might be 2 seconds or 10 seconds or more, and the length of time will vary from fish to fish. Too long a drop back and he's likely to mouth the bait, jump and spit it out. If the fish is bent on suicide and has crashed the bait, don't drop back at all.

On the other hand, if a fish is back there looking at the baits, but not eating, then don't swerve the boat, drop back, reel up or jig — just pray! But if he's back there for a few minutes, hasn't colored up, and you can't stand it any longer, speed the boat up or make a slight turn.

World's IGFA all-tackle record:

Atlantic Blue Marlin: Weight, 845 lbs. Length, 13′ 1″
St. Thomas, Virgin Is., 1968

Pacific Blue Marlin: Weight, 1,153 lbs. Length, 14′ 8″
Guam, 1969

Black Marlin

With an IGFA record of 1,560 pounds, here (together with the Pacific blue marlin) are the undisputed giants of the billfish family. Probably no other big game fish tests the total resources of the angler as does the black marlin.

You not only have to be in good shape physically, but willing to invest hard-earned money and time for a blue water safari. The fact is that almost without exception every angler fishing for black marlin is out to break the existing world's record. And they are willing to fly to Cairns, Australia, put up with fishing in winds up to 40 knots and spend $4,000 to $7,000 for a week's fishing!

You might ask, why Australia over Hawaii or Panama. The answer is because of the bunches of black marlin that seem to breed around the Great Barrier Reef. As a result, approximately 60 fish over 1,000 pounds have been caught on rod and reel in the last nine years. The take from commercial long-liners indicates that black marlin will grow to between 2,000 and 3,000 pounds.

In overall technique, fishing for black marlin is like going after blue marlin, except with blacks you've got an angry rhinoceros on your hands. And with all this weight they will jump, tailwalk, greyhound and sound! And when they do sound you've just about had it. For instance one fish was at the boat in ten minutes, then he jumped and sounded before the gaff could be put to him. As a result it wasn't until two hours and forty minutes later that the 1,239-pound monster was boated. Consequently speed is always in the back of your mind: you want the fish at the boat, wired, and gaffed as fast as possible.

Anglers from the U.S. have flown their bait to Mexico,

Panama, Canada, the Bahamas, etc., but not to Australia. One reason is that it is very costly to fly bait all the way to Australia, and then when you get there freezing facilities are minimal. However, the second reason is more important: there is a variety of excellent bait you can catch locally (and most of it quite similar to that used in the U.S. Except for a type of mullet caught "down under" called a blue tail, you will catch your own bait. For this purpose, the rig you use will be like the one used for blue runners in the U.S.; that is, a daisy chain of feathers spaced about 6 feet apart and fished 8 to 10 feet deep on a planer. Spoons are used for bonito, blackfin tuna and barracuda — all used as bait.

One of the best and most experienced black marlin men in the U.S., Mutt Coble, will tell you that if you want to produce these giants use scad. Scad is similar to our own mackerel, and you are going to want to choose one weighing about 1¼ pounds and belly rig him.

If you are using a blue tail mullet, then use one weighing ½ to ¾ pound and belly rig him, too.

When catching blackfin tuna or bonito cull the ones weighing about 5 pounds and head rig.

There is also a scaly mackerel that looks like a pot-bellied kingfish with a yellow tinge that makes a great bait and is sometimes used up to 20 pounds.

As a general rule of thumb, remember that all big baits or "splashers" are head rigged, while smaller baits are belly rigged.

For hooks you don't have to go over a 16/0, although some will use up to a 20/0. The big hooks have a disadvantage because they are very hard to drive in. The fact is, if you straighten the bend in a 12/0 or 14/0 Seamate you've got all the hook you need. Just make sure they're not single- or double-strength, but triple-strength hooks.

The size of the baits described are best for handling,

PHOTOGRAPH BY EMMETT R. "MUTT" COBLE

Black marlin.

hooking and trolling qualities, but at the same time you don't have to worry too much about size. The unofficial 1,805-pound black marlin swallowed a 150-pound Allison tuna! And even a 200-pound fish can easily take any bait you are likely to use. Just remember that the larger baits require a longer drop back. If you use a smaller bait than those suggested, the wahoo are likely to eat you up.

One word of caution when catching your own bait: Make sure to gut and salt immediately so he'll swim better and last longer.

The International Game Fish Association allows you 30 feet of double line to 30 feet of wire for line classes of 80 pounds and up. (While most black marlin can be taken on #80 line, you're after the all-tackle record, so use #130 line.) For leader you'll want to use about 24 feet of twisted #15 wire to a snap swivel, and then a short 6-foot leader of single strand #15 wire to the bait. In other words, your wire leader is in two parts.

John Erskin, Manager
Bransford holding head
rigged bonito.

Stanley Klaproth holds two
rigged scaly mackerel for
black marlin bait.

The reason for twisting the two wires together is to give you something more to grab onto when you are wiring the fish as well as to avoid clock springing the wire itself. The short wire helps to make the bait swim the way you want it to and is a lot faster to handle and store in the bait box.

When selecting line for black marlin fishing avoid dacron; use monofilament. Although dacron is excellent on smaller marlin, it has a tendency to snap on fish of a thousand pounds or more, whereas mono will stretch, giving you an extra advantage — which you are going to need!

As for the number of lines, you'll want to fish only two. The action is fast enough and three or four lines will just foul you up. For the same reason, use no teasers.

For a striking drag on 130-pound line use a "tuna drag" of 50-60 pounds. You are going to want to keep solid pressure on him because your concern is how fast you can get him to the boat to prevent him from sounding.

If you are going to fish out of Cairns itself, then you will have a 2½-hour run before you start trolling, or a loss of 5 hours fishing time a day. This means that the smart anglers sleep, eat and tie up to a mother ship already anchored out. You'll be fishing during Australia's winter months, or our late summer and fall. The prevailing winds blow off the Antarctic polar cap and are southeasterly, so be prepared for cool windy weather.

When you are actually fishing be on the lookout for current or surface "rips" in either clean or dirty water. Unlike blue marlin fishing, the clarity of the water is not a decisive factor with black marlin. They seem to feed wherever they want to and can be taken in 30 to 40 feet of water between the reefs, or bobbies, as they are called in Cairns. However, as a rule you'll be trolling in 20 to 50 fathoms for the bigger fish.

There are no weed lines to fish off the Great Barrier Reef but there are, unfortunately, Japanese long-liners. When you see the long-liners there are black marlin in the area, and when you don't you can bet fishing is dead because these billfish are the long-liners' bread and butter.

Almost everyone has heard about the tremendous number of sharks found on the Great Barrier Reef. This is not only a fact but to the angler it means you shouldn't fish too late in the day. The later it gets the greater the chances of your fish being lost to sharks.

Here is a final tip: A black marlin is going to be just as tough on the wire as he is on the line, almost as though he's never jumped at all. For this reason most men who wire these monsters take their cotton gloves to a shoemaker and have heavy leather sewn over the palms and the backs of them.

It is easy to see that to many men the black marlin represent the ultimate test of angler, boat, tackle and crew.

The season in Cairns starts on August 15 and runs until Christmas. Earlier than that the weather is too rough, and around Christmas the fish simply disappear and it's all over for the year.

By comparison to many other fishing areas, the number of charter boats available is small, so plan your trip many months (if not a year) in advance.

For reservations and information write to Mr. George Bransford, 72 Grafton Street, Cairns, N. Q., Australia.

World's IGFA all-tackle record:

Black Marlin: Weight, 1,560 lbs. Length, 14′ 6″
            Cabo Blanco, Peru
            August 4, 1953

White Marlin

Here is one of the most frustrating and challenging of all big game fish. He'll come up behind your baits and move from one to the other much faster than a blue marlin or sailfish, dancing around like he's crazy or has St. Vitus's dance. Not knowing which bait he's going to eat, the angler is kept jumping from rod to rod and back again. Although other billfish occasionally act this way, it is the trait of the white marlin.

As soon as he grabs the bait, he's likely to spit it out immediately, and then swim over to another bait, and then another. Whites have been known to stay behind a boat for five or six minutes, and then swim off without even eating!

Sometimes the action goes like this: A white comes up and mouths your bait, you give a normal drop back, then nothing. The same fish is back up a second time and you say to yourself, I am going to change my tactics and give him a "dip job." So you hold your rod tip up, now he takes the bait again; you dip your rod tip and raise it back up quickly, no drop back at all. And still you haven't hooked him!

Let's say this goes on for a while. You have had ten chances and he's eaten every bait in sight, except for the gill plates. At this point you say to yourself that you have had it, and start reeling in the gill plates or what's left of the bait. At this moment, he grabs what is almost a bare hook and you've got your fish! It has happened to more than one angler.

The white marlin is much sought after because he is not only a big fish, but a spectacular jumper. Ninety-nine percent of the time he will really light up, and he usually comes in on the bait this way. When you see the brilliant neon blue coloring his bill, tail, parts of his body,

97

PHOTOGRAPH BY CAPTAIN FRED S. HASTINGS

White marlin.

and especially his pectoral fins, he is usually ready to eat.

Here are some tips that will increase your chances of catching a white marlin. All sailfish baits are good for whites, but the preferred rig is a single hooked squid. Ballyhoo, mullet and strips are also excellent baits. Generally mackerel are too big, but occasionally a white will gobble a pound mackerel with relish.

For good results, skip or swim one of your baits straight down the center and troll along an edge. The edge in Bimini and Chub Cay, for instance, is where you see a sharp drop from 100 feet to 100 fathoms or more. Farther north in Ocean City, for instance, you troll along the fathom curves. Off of New Jersey and some other spots, it is areas like the "canyons" that produce the best. As far as season is concerned, the middle of March to the early part of May is best in Florida and the Bahamas; at other times of the year the fish move farther offshore. Since they seem to migrate, your best luck up north is later in the summer; for example, Ocean City is generally excellent in August.

An excellent white marlin bait: single hooked squid.

Whites, like blue marlin, will swim in bunches and in pairs. They are much more prevalent than blue marlin. As far as we know, Captain Fred Voss, Jr., holds the record, with twenty white marlin caught in one day! Sometimes they will chase free-swimming bait into a ball ("balling the bait") in Ocean City, much as sailfish do off of Stuart, Florida. When this happens the release and boated flags fly from every outrigger at the dock like the grand opening of a supermarket, which is the way it is when they ball the bait.

World's IGFA all-tackle record:

White Marlin: Weight, 159½ lbs. Length, 9'
Pompano Beach, Florida, 1953

PHOTOGRAPH BY AL RISTORI

Striped marlin.

Striped Marlin

Likely as not there is a man-o'-war bird circling high in the distance and, as you draw closer, you'll see a fish with the hump of his back and his sickle or top half of his tail out of water. Now you've spotted your first striped marlin off of Baja, California. What you're looking at is probably, pound for pound, the fastest and jumpingest of all marlin. A good size striped marlin can strip off 1,000 feet of line greyhounding across the water in one of the most spectacular sights in big game fishing. The striped marlin is found all over the Pacific Ocean, but some of the hot spots are lower California,

Pinas Bay off Panama, New Zealand and the Hawaiian Islands.

Whatever you've learned about fishing for other billfish generally applies to fishing for striped marlin. There are, however, two important differences: (1) you're going to hunt him, in calm weather at least, on the surface as you would for swordfish, and (2) he probably has more curiosity than any other billfish, which means you worry very little about spooking him. As a matter of fact, once you've got his attention you can on occasion actually tease him right up to the transom of the boat.

Sometimes they lie on the surface with their backs out of the water for so long their dorsals become dry and they seem almost unable to raise them. When they're like this they turn and come in on a bait like a shark does. At other times they come up under a bait and skyrocket upward, clearing the water by 6 or 8 feet!

Most of the time when he comes in on a bait he'll "color up"; his fourteen identifying vertical bars will shine a deep blue or purple and his pectoral fins will be straight out and rigid. One advantage in fishing for stripers is that they seem to be constantly hungry and if you get a bait near them, they'll eat!

For some reason the Pacific Ocean seems to have more bait fish than the Atlantic, or at least bait you can see on the surface. So along with man-o'-war birds, gulls and terns, look for big schools of sardines, anchovies and other bait. Chances are better that here you'll find striped marlin. And at times you'll see them balling the bait, particularly pilchards, as sailfish do in the Atlantic.

In terms of size, these game fish are larger than sailfish and white marlin, but smaller than blues or blacks; they average from 150 to 225 pounds but will grow to 500 pounds, possibly more.

When you've got one hooked you'll notice right away

Striped marlin.

that a striped marlin is a surface fighter; he rarely sounds. As a result they can be taken on very light tackle — even 12-pound test line is not uncommon — but the angler and crew really have to know what they're doing with this light stuff.

If you are a stranger to lower California, Pinas Bay or New Zealand, you are going to want to pick up any scent you can, that is, depth of water, underwater ridges and dropoffs, current, rips, birds, etc. While this is generally true, off of Baja you won't find rips. You'll just have to

An excellent striped marlin bait: split tail mullet.

hunt in deep water and, if the weather is bad, you'll have to blind troll until it clears. And off of Pinas Bay, Panama, for example, you have a very different situation. About 6 miles offshore and 10 or 12 miles southwest of Pinas Bay harbor you have peaks of underwater mountains that rise to within 200 feet of the surface and then fall off to tremendous depths. And due to the abundance of vegetation and plankton, the water is pea green in color. Apparently this isn't just a surface phenomenon but one that pervades the water to a good depth. As a result, the water is loaded with bait feeding on the plankton and the fish go hog wild with all this food around them.

Both Baja and Pinas have a good number of sharks; however, the food is so plentiful they rarely if ever grab a billfish. The same is true of cutoffs on your bait from barracuda. Once in a while a dolphin or rooster fish will grab your bait, but that is just about it as far as cutoffs are concerned.

For bait you can use mullet or ballyhoo if you take it with you. Locally, you'll want to use large (up to 18 inches) flying fish with either of the basic mullet rigs. Squid is also a natural food and an excellent bait for them, as are small bonito and mackerel. Live bait also works well but is unnecessary most of the time.

As for weather, the Pacific Ocean usually doesn't have the wind and consequently isn't normally as rough as the Atlantic: the seas usually consist of a big heave and are not really choppy. Off lower California the weather is generally cool and beautiful in January, February and March, and so, if possible, plan your trip for these months.

World's IGFA all-tackle record:

Striped Marlin: Weight, 415 lbs. Length, 11′
                Cape Brett, New Zealand
                March 31, 1964

PHOTOGRAPH BY JOHN R. CONNERS

Sailfish.

Sailfish

The sailfish is easily the most sought after and readily available of all billfish. His spectacular aerial acrobatics and his huge dorsal fin, or "sail," identify him around the world. He ranges the tropical or temperate oceans in abundance and will grow from a mere 6 inches to 6 feet in about one year!

There are concentrations of small sailfish in the Florida Keys in November and December each year, some weighing in as little as 12 ounces to 3 pounds. Off Palm Beach, Stuart and Fort Pierce, Florida, the best months are December, January and February. But make no mistake; they are caught from Central and South America to New Jersey, and may be taken year around.

As far as where to fish for them offshore, you want to fish the inside of the Gulf Stream and along the edge of the continental shelf. As you travel south through Ocean City, Maryland, and the Carolinas, troll along the fathom curves: then when you reach Florida you will find most fish taken closer to shore in 60 to 200 feet of water. As a matter of fact, at times you can hook sailfish a few hundred yards offshore at Palm Beach. There are two reasons for this: (1) the closeness of the Gulf Stream to land and (2) the narrowness of the continental shelf at this point. However, because the sailfish is a pelagic species they can be taken almost anywhere in blue water.

From many years' experience it is clear that weather affects your chances of catching sailfish. An onshore breeze is the best; when the wind is offshore the fishing is generally lousy. Also, you will want a light to medium chop on the water — even rough weather is preferred to a dead calm. To increase your chances when you're out, look for color changes in the water, tidal rips and seaweed lines to troll along.

Generally speaking, sailfish are hungry eaters and will bite more often than not. Sometimes you will find a "window-shopper," but there are many more occasions when you will get five or more chances at the same hungry fish. There are many stories about what you will see when a sailfish comes in on a bait. Here are some professional observations made over the years. Usually he comes in directly behind the bait and may or may not "color up." His bill may or may not be out of the water; the same is true of his big dorsal fin, although when he is ready to eat he will usually raise his sail somewhat. And he might or might not slap the bait with his bill.

For bait choose either a medium-size ballyhoo or a small 6- to 9-inch silver mullet.

Sailfish.

If you are going to use "bally," then use the standard ballyhoo rig with either a 7/0 or 8/0 hook.

With mullet use either the "slit back" or wedged and deboned rig. Make up some as "skippers" and some as "swimmers." And remember, it is always a good idea to keep a variety of baits out — that is, a ballyhoo, a mullet and a strip. Then if you start to get all your action on one kind of bait, switch all lines to troll that kind of bait.

Now here is the answer to the question asked most often: How do you hook a sailfish, how far do you drop back? Many will tell you to give the fish a long, long drop back, others will tell you to count to ten. Both suggestions, if followed, will put you far behind the angler who knows the following: Once the line comes out of the rigger pin, or your flat line is hit, put your reel immediately into free spool. Hold your thumb lightly against the line on the reel to prevent a backlash as he takes the line out on his initial run. Now, when you "feel" the fish carrying the bait your spool will speed up considerably. This is the time to put your reel in gear and if the line comes tight, he's there — *now* you set the hook.

As for setting the hook, many anglers get excited and actually snatch the bait out of his mouth, or break the line, when they should have hooked him. Remember, you want to drive the hook home with three or four jerks (quick pulls is probably more accurate).

But suppose you've done everything just right — you are in free spool, thumbing lightly, dropping back and "feel" the fish. Then you put the reel in gear and try him but he's not there, the line doesn't come tight. Don't drop back anymore, but just the opposite: reel back holding the tip of your rod directly over your head, or nearly so. Reel in enough line to bring the bait back up to where you can clearly see it in the water — and, more important, to see if the sailfish has come back to the bait. If you are too far back and can't see the bait, he's very likely to hit it again while you're in gear, causing you to miss your fish. Okay, now you've reeled back in where you can see the bait. Still holding the rod high, take the reel out of gear and hold your thumb on the spool, and more often than not he'll be right back on your bait giving you another chance at him.

Now when he hits the second time (or third, fourth, etc.) follow the same procedure: Drop back, "feel" the fish, line comes tight, set the hook. And your chances are excellent of catching the fish unless he's destroyed your bait.

The idea is to "feel" the fish on the drop back, and not to count to ten, fifteen or any other number!

The length of time (or drop back) between when he hits the bait and starts "carrying the mail" is going to vary with each attack as well as from fish to fish. And sometimes there is no drop back at all. For example, as with marlin, if he has crashed the bait and is obviously on, don't free spool at all.

Here's another tip that goes for any billfish. Let's say that you've dropped back, put the reel in gear, and he's not there — and then you see a billfish go immediately into the air. Now reel in as fast as you can because here

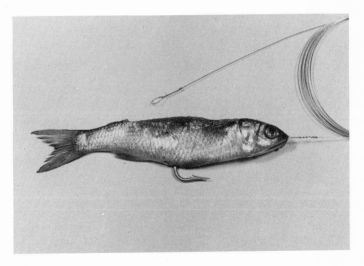

An excellent sailfish bait: slit back mullet rig.

is what happened: he originally took the bait and was hooked, but he's raced forward of where he grabbed the bait leaving you with a long loop of slack line. So you have to get the slack in and bring your line tight on him, or you are going to miss.

If you are going to live bait for sailfish — which is one of the most effective methods known to take them — then choose one of the smaller blue runners or goggle eyes in your bait well and troll very, very slowly so as not to kill (actually drown) your bait.

A word of caution: Sailfish are very dangerous to gaff since you have no control over his bill. Sailfish, and most white marlin, do not need to be gaffed. Just make sure that you've got a good wrap on the wire and grab his bill. Then, keeping his head down, let him have a couple or three good whacks with a billy club on top of his head and you've killed your fish.

While catching a sailfish takes some practice it is not as hard as it sounds, and seeing a sailfish tailwalk 50 or 60 feet across the top of the water, knowing he's on the other end of your line, is an experience well worth the effort!

World's IGFA all-tackle record:

Atlantic Sailfish: Weight, 141 lbs., 1 oz. Length, 8′ 5″
Africa, 1961

Pacific Sailfish: Weight, 221 lbs. Length, 10′ 9″
Galápagos, 1947

Swordfish

Swordfishing is a fever: to many an angler it is the ultimate in big game fishing. Not only is this due to the fact that they go well over 1,000 pounds, but also to the great difficulty in getting them to eat, although they are relatively easy to see when you are out hunting them. For example, in one year of tournament fishing, anglers off the northeastern coast of the United States only produced one fish caught on rod and reel!

The broadbill has been taken all along the East Coast of the United States, but the hot spots are off of Shinnecock in June, then east to Montauk, Long Island, in July and finishing up around Nantucket and Martha's Vineyard off Cape Cod in August and September.

How late you fish into September depends directly on the weather. You are going to want a nice day, preferring an absolute calm; rough weather makes swordfishing almost impossible. In a calm, when spotting from a tuna tower, you can see his sickle (dorsal) and tail on the surface. Swordfish have been taken while trolling, but the best way is to hunt and locate a fish first, and although you will generally only spot one fish, the chances are that there are more in the area. This means that you should check your fathometer when you do spot one. Let's say you see a swordfish in 30 fathoms of water. Well, then you are going to stay in 30 fathoms. These fish will stay in the same depth of water, sometimes for days at a time. They are usually captured in 20 to 100 fathoms of water.

Start looking in the shallower depths and then move out to deeper water. Weed lines, rips, and floating debris seem to make no difference at all, so forget them when swordfishing. It is, however, a good idea to follow the "stick" boats or commercial harpooners. At the same time, this can be frustrating because the commercial guys use small, spotter airplanes and are almost bound to reach a fish before you even have a chance to put your throttles in the corner.

Swordfish.

Some people will tell you that a jumping swordfish will not bite. Don't believe it! When you see one jump, go over as fast as your boat can move and take a look. Not long ago a 518-pound broadbill was taken following this simple rule rather than the old wives' tale.

Ninety-nine percent of the professional anglers and boat captains use squid as the preferred bait, with eels and the ubiquitous mullet weak second choices. Choose a 1- to 2-pound squid and use a single or double hook rig. Unless you are firm on your choice of a double hook rig, lean toward the single hook; it gives the fish a better chance of swallowing the bait. In any case use a 12/o Sea Demon hook and #15 wire, or two strands of #10 wire twisted together. Occasionally your fish will really mess up a leader and sometimes snap it; the twisted wire is helpful here because it cuts down on kinking. Cable is also used for leader material, but it is a little too obvious to the fish.

After you have spotted your fish, maneuver the boat slowly in front of him to present the bait. If there is a man in the tuna tower, let him hold the bait and line coming from the angler's rod in the cockpit. He can adjust the bait to the fish better than the men below. A swordfish wants a very slow-moving bait, so keep your speed way down and make sure your bait does not skip or splash. When he does hit, his whole body will light up an iridescent purple, although once in a while you will see a chocolate-colored one. These do not color up, but they are usually very big fish.

Although swordfish don't really "crash" a bait, they do have a slashing, vicious strike. When one takes your bait you want the boat dead in the water while you're free spooling on your drop back. As for the drop back, there are two theories: one says to drop back, and drop back, and drop back; the other, and preferred for all bill-fish, is to drop back until your reel picks up speed, or until you "feel" your fish. At this moment go full ahead on the engines and keep a tight line to hook the fish. If you miss the strike the fish may surface again, but usually that's it. You've got to go hunting again. And it is a hunt. A rough estimate is that, out of ten swordfish spotted, if you get two to bite you're lucky — and exceptionally lucky to land either one of them!

Here are several other thoughts to remember. Sword-

An excellent swordfish bait: double hooked squid rig.

fish don't jump very often but are spectacular when they do. And they are very mean at the boat. More than one has attacked a boat, and one even impaled himself on a submarine! So be very careful when he's at the boat. Use a light, striking drag because his whole body is tender, much more so than a marlin's. Also, as many swordfish are foul hooked as are fair hooked.

World's IGFA all-tackle record:

Swordfish: Weight, 1,182 lbs. Length, 14′ 11¼″
Chile, 1953

Bluefin Tuna

When you tie into a bluefin you are hooked up with the locomotive of ocean game fish. Although fewer anglers hunt the 300- to 900-pound giants than the smaller, schooling bluefin that are found off of Long Island, New York, for instance, either one is going to test the sheer physical strength and endurance of the angler.

These powerhouses generally follow the Gulf Stream north. They are caught off Bimini and Cat Cay in May and June and later on as they travel north off Barnstable, Massachusetts, and Provincetown, then on up in Nova Scotia and Newfoundland, and finally, Europe.

When you hook a bluefin he "smokes" your reel, and then goes down — straight down. Unlike billfish, the tuna always has a crashing strike. When he comes up to the bait that's it — you have either hooked him or missed him completely! Once in a while you see a loner or a pair, but tuna are generally found in schools of from 20 to 200 fish.

Giant tuna fishing is really a four-man job in the Bahamas: (1) one man in the cockpit to steer the angler's

Bluefin tuna.

Bluefin tuna.

chair, (2) the angler, and (3) and (4) the captain and a mate in the tuna tower, hunting. There are two men in the tower because you don't want to miss or lose the school. Once spotted the captain turns the boat ahead of the school, while the second man makes sure the fish are not lost in the sun, etc. The mate in the cockpit waits for an order from the tower to fire the bait overboard, which should come when the boat is in position ahead of the school.

There are three parts to fishing these monsters: (1) hunting the school, (2) presenting the bait, and (3) the hookup.

How far back you troll the bait depends on the wake of the boat. Tuna will sheer off of a wake rather than cross it, so the line is generally marked long, that is, well back of the wake. The less wake, therefore, the better. Because of the ledge you fish only one bait in the Bahamas — that is all you can handle. In "P" town you can fish two or three baits, no ledge. You will also find more blind trolling and the use of chum to lure fish up north.

Because the bluefin is on a northern migration, they are not feeding fish. Traveling fish are generally not searching for food. Sometimes you will see tuna busting bait, but they're not looking for it. The bait just happened to be in their migratory route.

The fact that the tuna are not feeding means that the swimming qualities and the presentation of the bait are of the utmost importance.

In the South mullet is the first choice of baits, with mackerel a close second; both are rigged as swimming baits. You want a bait weighing from 1¼ to 1½ pounds and as long as you can get — a skinny bait is best. For example, a 1¼-pound roe mullet might be 12 inches long, whereas a "road runner" might be 17 inches long. Use "road runners" when you can get them, and a belly rig to match.

In the north, say from Point Judith to Ipswich Bay, you will be doing a lot more blind trolling early in the season, and should have good luck using daisy chains made out of squid, mackerel or ballyhoo.

Later on you will be chumming with the boat either drifting or at anchor. In this case cut-up bunker or her-

An excellent bluefin tuna bait: split tail mullet.

ring are just about the best chum. One good method of chumming is throwing a hunk or two overboard, then wait until you can't see them in the water, then throw a few more pieces, etc. How much chum to use is pretty much up to you. For example, at one U.S. Atlantic Tuna Tournament, well over 100 boats have used tens of thousands of pounds of chum in as little as four days to produce just four fish. And other boats fishing a little further away produced two to five monsters each using as little as 10 to 20 pounds of chum.

It is generally best to rig your baits out of the same thing you're using for chum when fishing this way. This means take a whole or back half of a herring or bunker and put a hook in it, or hide it if you want to. Then just float your line out in the direction of your chum slick. Sometimes it is helpful to vary the depth of your bait by attaching a piece of styrofoam or a balloon to your line as a cork.

For these backbreakers you are going to need a triple-strength Seamate or Sea Demon 10/0 to 13/0 hook. To attach hook to leader use your same haywire twist to a barrel wrap but a heavy #15 wire, and always use tinned wire if possible. The coffee-colored wire just doesn't have the strength for the diameter.

One last question to answer and then you're on your own. People invariably ask how long it takes to put a giant bluefin in the boat. When he's hooked on the flats or in shallow water — and not able to get over the edge and sound — fish up to 600 pounds have been brought to "wire" in three to six minutes!

World's IGFA all-tackle record:

Bluefin Tuna: Weight, 1,065 lbs. Length, 10' 3"
                    Cape Breton, Nova Scotia
                    November 1970

Blackfin Tuna
(also False Albacore and Oceanic
or Arctic Bonito)

While these three species run smaller (average 6 to 10 pounds, but up to 40 pounds) than their big brothers, the Allison and giant bluefin, they should never be overlooked for several reasons. First, if you should capture a 40-pound blackfin, for instance, you would be a new world record holder. Secondly, they are not only tough

An excellent blackfin tuna and bonito bait: a trolling feather.

little fish but are found in such abundance that they can really make your day when nothing else is biting. And then, too, they make the finest strip baits in the world, which you can take home and freeze for another day.

The blackfin, false albacore and oceanic bonito are usually found in schools, sometimes numbering in the

PHOTOGRAPH BY AL RISTORI

Oceanic bonito.

thousands; this means plenty of fast action and lots of sport, especially on light tackle. It also means that where you find the schools you will usually find shark to challenge your heavier gear, and occasionally a blue marlin.

If the three advantages listed above need adding to, then realize that you troll for these fish strictly with spoons and feathers. Oh, they'll eat ballyhoo, mullet, strips and squid all right, but why waste the time and money when you do just as well with a ¼- to 1-ounce feather. If you are going to use feathers any color will do — yellow, red, white, red and white, etc. For spoons, get a small #1 or #2 Drone or Reflecto.

Also, you are going to want to troll a little faster for

all three species than you normally would for some of the other species of game fish.

When you are into a school of any one of these and you catch a small one, rig him as live bait and chances are nine times out of ten you'll be able to hook a shark, and sometimes a blue marlin.

World's IGFA all-tackle record:

Blackfin tuna: Weight, 38 lbs. Length, 3' ¾"
Bermuda, 1970

Oceanic bonito: Weight, 39 lbs. 15 oz. Length, 3' 3"
Walker Cay, Bahamas, 1952

Allison or Yellowfin Tuna

The Allison or yellowfin, like other tuna, is a powerhouse of sheer pulling strength. In fact, many agree that if he attained the weight of the giant bluefin he'd be the strongest swimmer in the ocean. These game fish are worldwide in distribution, but if your heart is set on Allison alone, then make a trip to the Bahamas in the spring of the year. During March, April and May Allisons are concentrated in great numbers in the islands. Two other hot spots are Bermuda in the fall and the Virgin Islands in the spring. However, a world's record was caught off Hawaii in 1962! And the current record was set in Mexico.

When you see a school of fish busting bait and clearing the water in great jumps, there is a good chance you are coming up to Allisons. When you see a tuna's dis-

Allison tuna.

tinctive shape and then the beautiful canary yellow on his finlets and filaments, dorsal and anal fin, you have found your game.

An excellent Allison tuna bait: trolling feather with a strip.

Allison or yellowfin are usually found in comparatively large schools of fish, or as singles and in pairs. But they may average between 100 to 200 pounds!

If you're going after Allison make your first choice of baits a trolling feather with a strip; next, trolling feathers on the head of a swimming mullet or ballyhoo. For rigging choose an 8/o or 9/o hook, and up to larger sizes if the fish are big. Even a baby 10-pounder will not have trouble with a 9/o, so stick with a large-size hook. Although Allisons are taken occasionally on skipping baits while marlin fishing, a swimming bait is always preferred for them.

These tuna are bait crashers, so if he misses your hook

on the first attack then jig the bait with your rod tip — don't reel up and don't drop back.

Since there is no drop back for striking Allison, you are going to use flat lines and pulled-down riggers to troll with. A pulled-down rigger means that your clothespin will be anywhere from one third to halfway up the rigger lines. Also remember to vary your trolling lines from, say, 50 to 100 feet behind the boat.

The following tip on trolling applies not only to Allison but to any surface-feeding fish: Don't run into the school or cross it, but stay on the edge of it and use a fast trolling speed.

World's IGFA all-tackle record:

Allison or yellowfin tuna: Weight, 296 lbs. Length, 6′ 9″
Mexico, 1971

Shark

From the cockpit you hear the cry "shark," and you turn your head just in time to watch the angler's prize dolphin or wahoo being attacked. This is all that "shark" means to the average angler — a destroyer of game fish. And this is true of more than 200 kinds of shark found in the oceans around the world.

But there are six species listed by the IGFA for world's records: the great white shark, the mako, porbeagle or mackerel shark, tiger shark, blue shark, and the thresher shark. These six, unlike all the rest, are game fish in their own right. The men and women who hold records on them can attest to their jumping ability and fighting characteristics.

Because of a legitimate fascination with their size and their teeth, as well as with their killing prowess, there are more books and movies on shark than anything else that swims. But unfortunately none is much help in telling you how to catch them.

Getting a big hook, a chunk of meat, and having some luck could snag one for you. However, like angling for other game fish, tipping the odds in your favor with a few facts and a little know-how will substantially increase your opportunities to capture one of these six.

First of all, these particular sharks are open ocean swimmers and are rarely found inside of the 100-fathom curve off the United States. Famous trolling areas are Montauk, Long Island, the Jersey shore, the Bahama Islands, all of Florida's eastern coast, England, Australia, New Zealand and Rockport, Maine!

The great white and the mako run pretty much as solo hunters, while the others like the blue shark will form packs at times. They can generally be found on the edge of migrating or schooling fish. They will show up off the grounds around Bimini at tuna time. Following their northerly migration, they will do the same thing with traveling schools of Spanish mackerel, herring and kingfish.

These are big animals with huge mouths so select 10/0 to 14/0 Sea Demon, Sobey, Seamate or Martu hook. For leaders use either cable or #15 tinned music wire as you would for bluefin tuna. IGFA regulations say you can use a 30-foot leader for 130- and 80-pound test line, and a 15-foot leader for 50 pounds and under.

Hunting a particular species of fish is almost always better than a "shotgun" approach; this means you choose

Shark.

your bait and rig to match the fish you're after. And while the spectacular mako loves to eat swordfish, other baits are cheaper and easier to get! And if anglers eat ham and cheese sandwiches, believe that any one of these sharks eats squid; make it one of your first choices of trolling baits. Following squid, use bonito, mackerel or mullet with belly rigs. Strip baits will also produce, particularly when cut from bloody fish such as bonito or blackfin tuna.

When you see a shark lazy on the surface and not feeding, get in front of him and then slip the baits overboard. It's all the better if you've got a bonito or tuna in the box to bleed over the transom into the wake of your boat. This will usually charge up his appetite and launch you into immediate action.

IGFA has regulations regarding lines, leaders and number of hooks, but what you use to *lure* the big ones is your own business. This means that when "sharking" chumming is legal. Except possibly for other sharks, any fish is good for chumming them. Better, however, are bonito, tuna, menhadden, herring, etc., for they are on his normal menu.

An excellent shark bait: double hooked squid.

The important thing to remember in chumming is to keep your chum line to the boat: this means that you hook up (anchor) if possible. Occasionally you can drift and chum in an area with little current on a calm day.

A last word. Sharks are potentially dangerous dead or alive. Dangling from a gin pole they will look dead but sometimes aren't; and even when they are, the slightest nudge or slip against their razor-edged teeth can cause severe, painful cuts. Take precautions: Tie them alongside of the boat for the trip home, tie them off on the gin pole, or turn them teeth down and shove them in the corner of the cockpit.

World's IGFA all-tackle record:

Great white: Weight, 2,664 lbs. Length, 16′ 10″
        Australia, 1959

Tiger: Weight, 1,780 lbs. Length, 13′ 10½″
        South Carolina, 1964

Mako: Weight, 1,061 lbs. Length, 12′ 2″
        New Zealand, 1970

Thresher: Weight, 729 lbs. Length, 8′ 5″
        New Zealand, 1959

Porbeagle: Weight, 430 lbs. Length, 8′
        England, 1969

Blue: Weight, 410 lbs. Length, 11′ 6″
        Rockport, Massachusetts

Wahoo

With speeds through the water exceeding 50 miles an hour, here's one of the fastest fish in the ocean. Combine this speed with more than 100 pounds of weight and you've got enough versatility to challenge any angler. Sometimes the wahoo crashes the bait like a blue marlin, and sometimes he'll skyrocket like a kingfish! Without a doubt he is stronger and faster than a kingfish, but like his brother mackerel, he will chop your bait off about half the time unless you are wisely using a double or triple hook rig.

If after two or three runs of a hooked fish your rod begins to vibrate with a series of staccatolike jerks, then chances are there is a wahoo on the other end. What is happening is that he's violently shaking his head to throw the hook, and this action is telegraphed straight

An excellent wahoo bait: double hooked strip with trolling feather.

up the line to you. If St. Vitus's dance is characteristic of the white marlin, then the shaking head identifies the wahoo. And like billfish, the wahoo will "color up" — his vertical bars will light — and usually he either stays colored up or lights up again when he's brought to the wire.

Wahoo are caught all year 'round and they do seem

PHOTOGRAPH BY CAPTAIN FRED S. HASTINGS

Wahoo.

to migrate. From the middle of February to the middle of April, they are concentrated from Bimini to Walker's Cay and around to Green Turtle Cay in the Bahamas. Then up to Oregon Inlet off North Carolina in July, and even farther north to Ocean City, with a few taken off Montauk, Long Island.

Wahoo don't really school like kingfish, but there are occasions when you'll be fishing four lines and get four wahoo, and as soon as they're boated, you put your lines back out and get four more.

131

Just about in this order, the preferred baits are: (1) a feather with a strip, (2) ballyhoo, and (3) mullet. Although he will take skipping baits, rigging your baits to swim will increase your chances.

If you are going out strictly for wahoo (which would be a little unusual), then fish all baits from the flat — no outriggers, no drop back. If you want to troll four baits, keep your outriggers down as far as possible; that is, run your clothespins up only enough to keep your lines separated. And if you miss him the first time, jig your line as you would for kingfish.

One last word to help you boat your wahoo. When you're bringing your fish to wire keep your boat at trolling speed, or even go a little faster. The reason for this is that a wahoo is particularly likely to make one last run ahead of the boat as you bring him alongside. If you let him get away with this he's likely to charge underneath the boat, or get headway and double back throwing slack in the wire and then coming tight and snapping it.

World's IGFA all-tackle record:

Wahoo: Weight, 149 lbs. Length, 6′ 7¾″
Cat Cay, Bahama Islands, 1962

Kingfish

There is usually a short two-week run of kingfish off Florida's eastern coast in August, but the real season is December through March, sometimes extending into

PHOTOGRAPH BY CAPTAIN FRED S. HASTINGS

Kingfish.

the first week in April. A school from ½ mile wide to 5 miles long has been known to stay in just about the same location for these months, bringing the commercial man a living and the sportfisherman week after week of furious, bone-tiring action. Don't worry about the commercial man ruining your fun; he not only uses a hook and line as you do but aids you every day since he usually leaves at daybreak and has the school located before you've finished breakfast.

Kingfish are talked about in two ways: (1) "snakes," running from 3 to 10 pounds, and (2) "smokers," going from 25 to 50 pounds and more.

133

For school kings or "snakes" use a spoon, feather, or whole ballyhoo. If you watch the commercial men near you, you'll see them constantly jigging their hand lines. Do the same thing with your rod tip from time to time

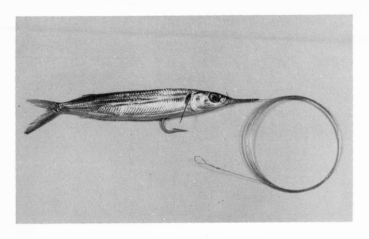

An excellent kingfish bait: ballyhoo.

to pick up more fish. With whole ballyhoo, drift or troll as slow as you can over the school. Sometimes the fish are deep; then what you do is troll in a slow, sharp circle to drop your spoon or feather deeper, even going to a trolling plane if necessary. When using ballyhoo, make up some double hook and triple hook rigs and just slap the bait on. When kingfish are feeding you don't need special trolling baits; just make sure you get the hooks in the bait and the bait overboard.

"Smokers" are bigger and trickier. First of all, except for live bait, you are going to troll very slowly and way, way back of the boat, between 200 and 250 feet.

For "smokers" any live bait is preferred, next a rigged dead goggle eye or blue runner. So keep the ones that die in your live well, because they're second choice to the live ones for big kings. If you don't have either of these, then use mullet rigged with two hooks. Pick a fairly large mullet, at least ¼ pound. Another good choice of trolling baits is a giant ballyhoo, the biggest you can buy: cut out the backbone and rig with double or triple hooks.

World's IGFA all-tackle record:

Kingfish: Weight, 78 lbs., 12 oz. Length, 5' 5½"
Dominican Republic, 1971

Dolphin

Pound for pound the dolphin is probably as strong as a sailfish; he's a jumper that will give you plenty of thrills before you bring him to gaff.

Dolphin are found around the world. They are caught off New Jersey and are thick off Cape Hatteras, North Carolina, in June, and in the Bahamas' Tongue of the Ocean you can walk on them in April. The world's record was caught off Spanish Wells in the Bahamas, but this is waiting to be broken wherever you find blue water.

The dolphin's jumping ability, the speed of his runs and excellent food qualities, when combined with the beauty of his colors, make him a truly universal game fish throughout the world.

The preferred bait is ballyhoo. For dolphin don't buy small or giant ballyhoo, but get a medium-size ballyhoo and use a single 7/o hook with the basic ballyhoo rig.

Other good baits are strips and feathers. A strip bait has the advantage of being relatively weedless, which is

Dolphin.

helpful because you will be trolling around weeds when you can. Dolphin will also readily take feathers, and while they will take any color, stick with yellow. Whether you use a skirt or feather in front of the strip is strictly up to you. Mullet are also frequently used and produce well.

Floating patches of weeds, logs, orange crates — any

flotsam and jetsam — are good bets for finding dolphin. Some say that the floating debris provides shade for the dolphin. This seems hard to believe because one orange crate might have fifty good-size dolphin around it! It seems more likely that the debris provides at least some protection for tiny bait fish.

You will notice that striking dolphin almost always cross behind the boat to take a bait. This is because you are generally trolling along the debris or weeds and not through them, rather than because of any peculiarity of the fish. They will, however, charge the bait on the surface the majority of the time; this is characteristic of the dolphin.

When you are "bailing" school dolphin, keep one overboard until you hook another one to keep the school by the boat, then bring in the first and keep the second one out until you hook the third, and so forth. In this way you will keep the main body of fish by the boat. Here are a few tips to help you load up. First, shorten up on your leader to 2 or 3 feet so you can really throw them in the fish box. Next, use a smaller 5/0 hook and chunks of bait. Don't use a whole ballyhoo or even a half, just drift a chunk overboard. And don't lose too many or the school will leave; this means when you're putting them in the boat don't snatch too hard.

If the school does leave because you've lost too many or shark have moved in, then get rerigged with your regular trolling baits. Go back by the weed patch or wherever you first caught them, and when they come back start the whole procedure over again.

School dolphin generally run from 1 to 3 pounds or thereabouts, but there is also a good chance a pair of 15- to 20-pounders are in the area, so don't be surprised if your reel suddenly starts to smoke. With a big bull dolphin, you want to hook him right away because they have been known to eat every bait trolled and take every hook if the angler is slow, which means you have one heck of a mess on your hands and might lose a record fish as well.

The best method of gaffing almost any fish is to keep his head in the water as you wire him. This is particularly

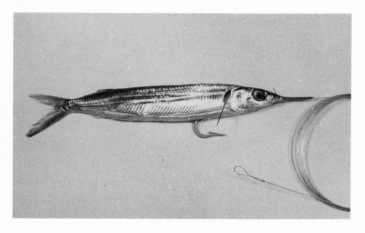

An excellent dolphin bait: single hooked ballyhoo.

true of dolphin because the minute his head is out of water he's going to jump, and chances are he'll throw the hook or break the leader.

World's IGFA all-tackle record:

Dolphin: Weight, 85 lbs. Length, 5′ 9″
Spanish Wells, Bahamas, 1968

Barracuda

The great barracuda, or simply "cuda," is larger than his Pacific Ocean cousin and has blinding speed for short distances. And while he is called a lot of different names, a "starter-fish" is appropriate for those who are new to big game fishing; this is particularly true for those who are fishing without professional assistance. The reason barracuda make a good starter-fish is they will hit almost any bait, spoon, or feather you rig up, and they are recognized by the International Game Fish Association.

As far as fighting qualities are concerned he hits quickly, more often than not hooks himself, and then puts up a fierce but very short fight. Because they are

An excellent barracuda bait: ballyhoo with trolling feather.

numerous, and can be caught from right on shore to blue water, they offer an excellent opportunity to gain valuable experience in rigging baits, using your tackle, fighting game fish, and actually putting one in the boat.

Barracuda.

The preferred rigs are double or triple hooked strips, mullet or ballyhoo. A swimming bait will catch more than a skipping one. The great majority of the time he will either cut your bait off or hook himself. If he cuts your bait and does not get hooked, then jig as you would for kingfish.

There are very few fishermen who do not know that a barracuda has a mouth full of very large and very sharp teeth. This means that you are going to use a wire leader and be very careful when handling the fish. If because of size you have to gaff him, then make it good, just behind the head, and keep his teeth away from you until he's safely in the fish box. On smaller fish simply hold him up by the wire leader and then slide your other hand up under his gill plates and grab him by the throat latch; this is really the safest way to handle him.

World's IGFA all-tackle record:

Barracuda: Weight, 83 lbs. Length, 6′ ¼″
        Africa, 1952

Rybovich Sportfisherman underway.

9.

Angling Techniques

H ow you handle your boat and where you troll is going
to make a considerable difference in what you bring
back to the dock or release. Very simply, trolling is a
skill. It is not so much fishing from a boat, as some sug-
gest, as fishing *with* a boat.

Hooking a swordfish, for example, requires that you
know when the boat should be dead in the water and
when the throttles should be in the corner to hook him.
Getting a giant bluefin tuna means two men in the tuna
tower and two in the cockpit coordinating the boat-

handling and the presentation of bait. On almost any blue water fish the handling of the boat, more often than not, can mean the difference between whether or not you bring fish back to the dock. And then, of course, there is when, how, and where to troll.

So when you are headed for blue water, remember that your boat is going to make a great contribution in (1) locating the fish, (2) keeping your baits swimming or skipping, and *not* spinning, and (3) hooking and boating your fish.

Locating the Fish

Blue water is not just another term for the ocean, but is an observable fact: some water appears pale green because it is shallow, clear, and the bottom growth reflects upward; some water is brown with silt or pollution; some water is deep green or even reddish because of algae or plankton — but blue water is a clear, deep blue. And the fantastic clarity of the water, rather than the blueness, is its most distinctive characteristic.

Most of the time you are going to locate more fish and be more productive in blue water.

Some will tell you they have caught fish in 1,000 fathoms of water or more. True, but generally they don't mean out in the middle of the open ocean. What they do mean is that they trolled along very sharp drop-offs such as you find in Bermuda, Hawaii, the Cayman Islands, the Bahamas, and the Seychelles of the Indian Ocean, or along the edge of the continental shelf of the U.S. Except for the shelf, all are really the tops of underwater mountains and so abound in bait fish and all marine life, including the big game fish you are after.

Much the same is true of the fathom curves on your marine charts, and the "canyons" off of New York and New Jersey. These are really elongated pits, or deep indentations in the ocean floor, serving much the same purpose as a dropoff.

With this in mind, then, to locate fish, look for the following changes in the otherwise endless stretches of blue water:

1. Change in depth or dropoffs, "canyons" and underwater mountains, the fathom curves from Ocean City south, and the inside edge of the Gulf Stream in Florida.

2. Changes in water color from almost any color to true blue water: watch for tidal rips. Troll these edges.

3. Changes in water surface, including seaweed lines, floating patches of weeds, and floating debris.

4. Changes in water temperature; for example, stay along the colder side of a surface temperature drop of, say, from 70 to 75 degrees to 64 to 68 degrees, and fish it as you would a weed line.

5. Changes in the wind and waves. An onshore breeze is best with a medium chop, and rough weather is preferable to a dead calm for most blue water game fish.

6. Changes in weather lasting from a few days to more than a week. For example, any northeaster will increase the capture of game fish along Florida's eastern coast. But the same is true of fish all over the world; that is, a particular and strong onshore wind will increase your chances of producing fish.

Here is a last observation on "change" on which you will have to make up your own mind. While it is true that tarpon and kingfish, for example, like a full moon, your blue water game fish seem to prefer the darker phases of the moon, even though you are fishing during the day! This observation comes from experience and seeing the landings at dockside rather than from any scientific proof. Commercial snapper fishing at night is offered as further "proof." Hand lining for yellowtail snapper on Matenella reef and through the Florida Keys has proved over and over again that the phases of the moon make a big difference. For yellowtail at night, the darker phases always outproduce the lighter phases of the moon. And in St. Thomas a full moon is hot for billfishing.

Keeping Your Bait Swimming or Skipping

First of all, make sure your bait is rigged properly and that your hooks are neither binding nor hanging too loosely from wherever you've positioned them. To make sure of this, put your baits out a short distance behind the boat and watch them awhile before running them up on the riggers or letting them out on the flat lines.

Since all of this is one operation, whoever is driving the boat should maintain whatever speed is necessary to keep the baits swimming or skipping. When the baits are rigged correctly then one speed is all that's necessary. You do not need more RPMs for skipping and less for swimming baits, or vice versa.

As you might well know, the number of RPMs to reach a given speed varies considerably from boat to boat, so when you get your bait to swim right look at your tach and use those RPMs for openers. Remember also that your trolling speed will vary with sea conditions, as well as how far behind the boat you troll the baits. For instance, when you have fairly rough weather, a longer rigger line will likely be necessary to get your bait to swim or skip correctly without jumping. A rule of thumb is that you want to troll slower in choppy water, or lengthen your lines and drop your riggers some. As for how far back to troll your baits, it is a very good idea to keep your baits close enough to the boat to see them. In this way you can see your baits and any fish that might come up to them.

Hooking and Boating Your Fish

Here we are going to consider tackle only briefly because what you use is between you and your local bait and tackle dealer. There are, however, a few suggestions that any big game angler and charter boatman will agree with. First of all, buy the best tackle you can afford. It will save you unnecessary physical strain when fighting a fish, will last for years if properly cared for, and should not break, jam or fly apart in the middle of a battle. Next buy balanced tackle, matching rod, reel and line. Don't for example put a 6/o reel on a 20-pound rod, or load a 4/o reel with 80-pound monofilament. If you are unsure about matching tackle, then let your local tackle dealer help you. Finally, don't overtackle or undertackle. It looks more than a little silly to go after sailfish with a 10/o reel and an 80-pound rod fishing 130-pound test line. On the other hand, ultralight tackle is absurd on giant bluefin tuna.

So if your tackle is right, the bait is right, your boat-handling is right, and you've located your fish, then it's a question of getting him to strike, hooking him and boating him.

In general it is better to hunt a given species of

big game fish rather than use a scattered, or shotgun, approach. At the same time it is recognized that most anglers will set out for a billfish and pick up dolphin, kingfish, bonito, etc., even though they are rigged specifically for billfish. However, when you hunt for a given species you do some things quite differently. For example, to get a kingfish to strike you troll very slowly. When you are in a school of dolphin, you are going to leave one overboard to keep the school near the boat to load up. For giant bluefin tuna, correct presentation and its position with respect to the boat's wake are very important. If you are after wahoo, then you do better on flat lines than you do on outriggers. Blackfin tuna and false albacore both require faster trolling speeds. On marlin you are going to want to pull your throttles back to idle when the fish knocks the bait out of the outrigger. This is because it will give you a more natural drop back and at the same time continue to give your other baits some action. For a more complete discussion turn to the specific fish in your *Blue Water Bait Book*.

With the exception of billfish, most fish will hook themselves, but remember to drive the hook home when you grab the rod. It's good insurance. On billfish the one technique that most often puzzles anglers is how far to "drop back" or let him run with the bait before striking him. The answer is this: When the fish strikes the bait put the reel into free spool immediately. At the same time hold your thumb lightly against the line on the reel to prevent a backlash. Next, the spool on your reel will speed up considerably as you "feel" the fish carrying the bait. This is the time to put your reel in gear, crank, and when the line comes tight, set the hook. The amount of drop back on billfish is going to vary from fish to fish; some need long drop backs, some short ones, and some none at all. This means that other suggestions on drop back such as counting to ten or fifteen don't always work, whereas watching or feeling the speed of your spool as the fish runs with the bait is the best method.

In any event, the man operating the boat can always speed up and help the angler hook his fish, if he watches the angler's rod and times it just right so as not to take the bait away from the fish. Realize, too, that some fish are bent on suicide, and then your problem is not hooking him but only landing him.

Your reel drag is also very important in hooking your fish (and protecting your equipment). For a striking drag try to use about one third the breaking test of your line, i.e., on 30-pound test set your striking drag at about ten pounds over the rod tip. Put a man in the fighting chair, or have him standing with a gimble belt, and attach the line from the tip to any good hand spring scale to test the drag.

When a fish such as a marlin or wahoo makes a sizzling run, back off to about half of the striking drag to avoid snapping the line. Remember, it is not only the fish that puts a strain on the line, but when you have 250 to 350 feet of line out water friction puts a big additional strain on the line. The suggestion for backing off on the drag when the fish is really "carrying the mail" is a good one, but the better the angler the closer he can come to putting the drag on the "corner" if the fish is settled down. By this is meant that some anglers can go to possibly 75 pounds of drag while fishing 80-pound test line.

To fight the fish keep your rod at a normal 45-degree angle and pump slowly up and as fast down as you can without giving slack. Pumping is simply using your back, legs and arms to raise the rod, then reeling in line as you lower it, then raising it again, and so forth.

Here's one last tip for you when fishing new waters.

Use your charts to locate dropoffs, fathom curves, etc., and talk with your bait and tackle dealer before leaving the dock. Then watch and listen to other boats when you are out.

While what is said here is accurate and will help you capture more fish, angling is still an art and depends on experience, so once you have been in the fighting chair and caught a few, all of this will become more meaningful to you.

10.

Special Cockpit Equipment

There are few things more important to successfully fighting a big game fish than the leverage given the angler. It is doubtful if there is a man in the world strong enough to land a giant tuna or a big marlin without the aid of a harness or fighting chair, not only because of the strain on the angler from the weight of the rod and reel and the constant pull of the fish against the reel drag, but also due to the twisting and turning of an unsupported rod as the fish jumps and sounds.

What follows are some of the aids that a professional angler would have on board. Also included is some of

Boating a blue marlin with gin pole tackle and meat hook.

the equipment for boating these monsters. It is quite obvious to most that fish weighing up to 1,500 pounds require something more than a strong pair of arms to put them in the cockpit. So whether it is a gin pole, tuna door or flying gaff, your familiarity with the equipment, what it is and how to use it, is essential.

While the following pages will give you a quick glimpse of the equipment involved, there is no substitute for seeing your tackle dealer about your particular needs. What you require will vary considerably according to the amount of cockpit space available and the type of fishing you are going to do. Money, too, is a factor. A good bucket harness can run over $100 and a custom fighting chair well over $1,000. But don't get discouraged; good used equipment is changing hands all the time.

Remember, too, that it is wise to take a look at other fishing boats. Because much of the equipment is custom-made, the placement of it, how it's fastened down, etc., take considerable planning. And so if someone else has a good working layout, use it!

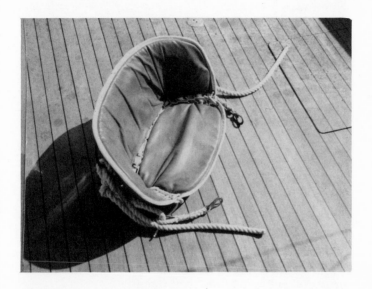

Bucket or Kidney Harness. These harnesses are a must in fighting giant tuna or big marlin. They allow the angler to use his legs to do the heavy work. Because the rod, when fighting a fish, is in the gimbal of the fighting chair and the harness is hooked to the reel, both arms and hands are free to rest from time to time. The adjustable straps that come with these harnesses are often discarded in favor of dacron or nylon line as pictured. The line is simply easier to adjust and has less bulk than the straps. The harness is adjusted to fit both the angler and the angle of the rod. For example, in tuna fishing you want the rod to be almost vertical. The bucket harness is really nothing more than a kidney harness with a seat attached so as to prevent the harness from riding up the angler's back.

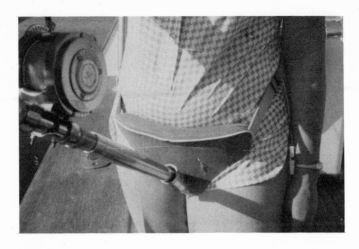

Fighting belt with gimbal. This is worn when you stand up to fight a fish. Without it you would be forced to hold the rod butt in your stomach or between your legs. For rods without gimbal butts a belt is made with just a leather cup, no gimbal.

Shoulder harness. When used with a fighting belt as pictured above, you can use your back in a standup fight. When used in the chair on big fish you have to have a very strong back. For this reason most anglers prefer a bucket harness.

Custom fighting chair. Chair can swivel 360 degrees and has adjustable footrest, adjustable backrest, and slotted armrests with rod holders below; also a reversible gimbal to fit either straight or curved rod butts. Cost of custom chair can run as high as $1,500.

Three fighting chairs. Picture shows usual placement in cockpit. Smaller chairs have 360-degree swivel, gimbal and one rod holder. Smaller chairs are fine for sailfish, dolphin, blackfin tuna, etc. All chairs lock into any position desired for traveling or dockside convenience.

Fighting chair. Picture shows slotted armrest with curved rod butt in rod holder. Safety line is attached to armrest and ring on bottom bracket of reel.

Tuna door. Picture shows tuna door cut into transom of boat. When done correctly the door doesn't weaken the structure of the boat at all. The door is the easiest way of all to put a really big fish in the boat. Make sure door is both big enough and low enough; if too small it's useless.

Gin pole. Picture shows gin pole with block and tackle. Block ratio is usually 3:1 or 4:1. The pole itself is usually built high enough above the gunwale so you can swing the fish over it and into the boat. Although some boats have both a gin pole and a tuna door, a gin pole is generally used when for one reason or another a tuna door isn't possible.

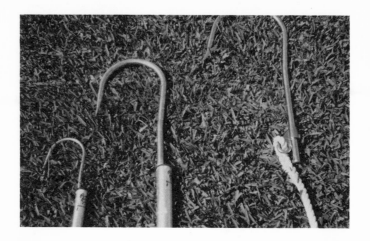

Three gaffs. Left to right: 4-inch hook for kingfish, wahoo, dolphin, etc. Next, eight-foot tuna gaff for taking bluefin. When you "stick" a tuna, that's usually it. It has no barb on its head so if you get a bad gaff you can get it out and take another bite. Next, a flying gaff for marlin, swordfish, etc.

Flying gaff. Picture shows unloaded flying gaff with 25-foot nylon line spliced to gaff head. Head is flattened, sharpened and barbed. Hook fits into slot of handle. When loaded, line comes up over end of handle and line is secured to base of fighting chair.

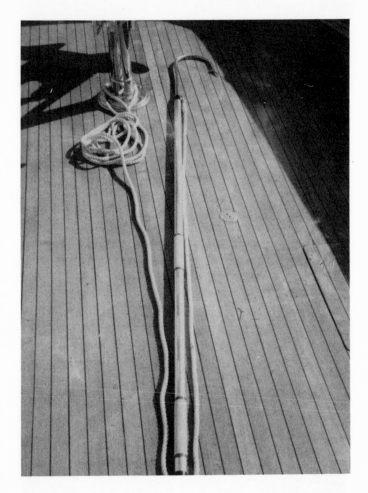

Flying gaff. Picture shows gaff ready to use. Handle is really only a guide and base for the gaff hook. Most of your pull is on the nylon line when you gaff. Make sure you gaff over the back and under the backbone, not in the soft underbelly, if possible. As soon as you gaff the fish, pull handle loose and put in cockpit.

Tail rope. 15 to 25 feet of line spliced with loop on one end and snap on other end. Wire cable core on snap end of line to help tail rope sink. While fish is in the water, snap rope over leader, then move back over head to tail.

Billy club. Here's a commercially made club, but whether they're homemade or cut from a hunk of iron pipe, you're going to need something to quiet the fish down. Hit him above the eyes where his brain is. Be careful not to bust your fingers or someone else's when you do it.

Meat hook. This one explains itself. It is usually stuck in the lower jaw of a fish, and is especially helpful in pulling a big one through the tuna door.

Appendix

International Game Fish Association

Rules Governing Record Catches

All IGFA angling rules are voted on by the officers, executive committee, international committee, and angling clubs with current IGFA membership status. Records are only kept on marine species.

All claims for an IGFA world record catch must be approved by at least two officers or members of the executive committee before being acknowledged as a world record.

Questionable or protested applications for world records will be referred to the full executive committee. Such catches will be removed from the chart until a decision is reached.

No claim will be considered unless it is accompanied by the correct amount and kind of line sample.

In case of a disputed identification two competent ichthyologists will be called upon to make the decision. If there is a question, the angler will be notified and given ample opportunity to send in further identification.

In some instances, an officer or member of an IGFA committee or a deputy from a local member club may be asked to recheck information supplied on a claim. Such action is not to be regarded as doubt of the formal affidavit, but is merely an evidence of the extreme care and accuracy with which the IGFA tries to maintain its world record charts.

To replace a record for a fish weighing 100 pounds or more, the replacement must weigh at least one pound (16 ounces) more than the existing record. A catch exceeding the existing record by less than one pound will be considered a tie with the existing record. In case of a tie claim involving more than two catches, weight must be compared with the *lowest* weight involved in the existing records, but nothing *less* is a claim.

To replace a record for a fish weighing less than 100 pounds, the replacement must weigh at least one-half pound (8 ounces) more than the existing record. A catch exceeding the existing record by less than half a pound will be considered a tie with the existing record.

No estimated weights will be accepted.

Time Limit on Claims

Claims for fish caught in continental U.S. waters will not be accepted by the International Game Fish Association if the date of the catch is more than 60 *days* before the date of receipt of the claim by the IGFA. Claims for fish caught in other waters will not be accepted if the date of the catch is more than *three months* before the date of receipt of the claim by the IGFA.

If a claim for a record is entered without full particulars, a period of two months is allowed during which the IGFA shall make an effort to complete the claim, and after which time, if the claim still remains incomplete, the catch shall be discarded as a claimant for a record.

When a new species of fish is made eligible for a record, the date of the announcement will be the effective date, and time limit on claims will be as of that date. No prior catches will be considered. Appearance of the name of such a fish upon the record chart for the first time will be considered proper notification in lieu of any other notice.

Scales

All record fish should be weighed on scales that have been checked and certified for accuracy by government agencies or other qualified and accredited organizations. All scales should be checked and certified at least once each six months.

If at the time of weighing the fish, the scale has not been properly certified within six months, it should be checked for accuracy as quickly as possible, and a report included with the application *stating the findings* of the inspector prior to any adjustments of the scale.

If a properly certified scale is not available, the scale must be checked by weighing objects of recognized and proven poundage. This type of weight check must be at least equal to the weight of the fish. Any type scale may be used as long as its accuracy can be established.

No fish weighed only at sea will be accepted as a claim for an IGFA record.

A fish must be weighed by an official weighmaster, if one is available, or by a recognized local or IGFA official. Disinterested witnesses to the weight should be used whenever possible.

At the time of weighing the actual tackle used must be exhibited to the weighmaster and weight witness.

No estimated weights will be accepted.

Preparation of Record Claims

Record applications will only be accepted for the class of line actually used in catching the fish. If the line overtests, the application will be considered in the next higher class. If the line undertests into a lower class, the application will not be considered for the lower line class. The highest pound test line permissible is 130-pound class. If the line test on an all-tackle claim overtests 130 pounds, it will be considered as an all-tackle record only and will be listed as such if approved.

The angler must fill in all items on the application personally, and the association urges that the angler send in his own affidavit, line sample and photographs. The line sample should be submitted in a manner that it can be unwound without damage to the line. A recommended method is to take a rectangular piece of stiff cardboard and cut a notch in opposite ends. Secure one end to the cardboard and wind the line on the cardboard in the notched areas. Secure the other end and identify it. Also, place your name on the cardboard. Do not submit the line in a hank.

Extreme care should be exercised in measuring the fish, as the measurements are usually important for other scientific studies.

The angler is responsible for seeing that the necessary *signatures* of boat captain, weighmaster and witnesses are on the claim. If an IGFA officer, or member of the IGFA executive or international committee, or officer of a member club is available, he or she should be asked to witness the claim. The name of a boatman, guide, or weighmaster repeated as witness will not be acceptable.

The application form must be used in filing claims and must be accompanied by the mandatory yardage (see Angling Rules) of actual line used. The application form may be reproduced. The application form and line sample originally submitted will be the only one considered. It is of the utmost importance that application forms be filled in carefully and correctly.

The angler must appear in person to have his application notarized. In territories where notarization is not possible or customary, the signature of a government commissioner or resident, a member of embassy, legation or consular staff, or an officer or member of the executive or international committee of the IGFA may replace notarization.

Any deliberate falsification of an application will disqualify the applicant for any future record!

Photographs

Photographs of the fish, the rod and reel used to make the catch and the scale used to weigh the fish shall accompany each record application. A photograph of the angler with the fish is also desired. Shark photographs should also include a photo of the head and the nature of the front teeth. Enough pictures must be submitted to identify the species without a doubt. This is especially important with the marlin, bass, shark, and tuna species.

Photographs should be taken of the fish in a hanging position and also lying on a flat surface on its side. In both types of photograph, no part of the fish should be obscured. When hanging, the fish should be broadside to the camera with all fins, tip of the jaws, sword or spear clearly shown. Do not hold the tip of any fin. Do not stand in front of the fish; also do not hold the fish.

When photographing a fish lying on its side, the surface beneath the fish should be smooth and a ruler or marked tape placed beside the fish if possible. Photographs from various angles are most helpful. An additional photograph of the fish on the scale and showing the weight helps in expediting the application.

Angling Rules

1. Any fish caught by any method of fishing in accordance with IGFA rules is eligible for a record claim if it outweighs the existing record by the required amount in its line class. The rod, reel and all other tackle must be in reasonable proportion, or "balance" to the line size.

2. The IGFA record classes are: all-tackle (an all-tackle record is the heaviest fish caught on any of the line classes listed); 6-pound line class (line testing up to and including 6 pounds); 12-pound line class (line testing more than 6 pounds and up to and including 20 pounds); 20-pound line class (line testing more

than 12 pounds and up to and including 20 pounds);
30-pound line class; 50-pound line class; 80-pound
line class; 130-pound line class.

3. Record classes are based on the wet testing strength
of the actual line used in making the catch. All line
testing is conducted in a nationally recognized labora-
tory in accordance with Spec. CCC-T-191b, Method
4102.

   All claims for records in line classes less than 50
pounds must be accompanied by 50 feet (including
the entire double) of the actual line used in making
the catch. For line classes of 50 pounds or more, 80
feet (including the entire double) must be submitted.
The line sample must be in one piece.

   Backing: If two lines of different test strength,
spliced or tied together are used in taking a fish, that
catch shall be classified under the heavier of the two
lines and a sample of both lines must be submitted.

   NOTE: The IGFA tests lines only in connection
with applications for records.

4. The leader and the double line on all weights of
tackle up to and including the 50-pound line class,
shall be limited to 15 feet of double line and 15 feet
of leader. For heavier tackle, the line shall not be
doubled at the leader end for more than 30 feet, and
the leader shall not exceed 30 feet. There are no
minimum lengths. Also, the use of a double line or
leader is not required. The length of the leader shall
be the overall length including any legal hook arrangement attached thereto. A double line must be
the doubling of the actual line used. The leader may
not be lengthened to compensate for a shorter
double, and the double line may not be lengthened
commensurately for a shorter leader. The double line

and the leader must be connected with a knot, snap or a swivel. There are no limits to the material or strength of the leader. When the leader is brought to within the grasp of the mate, or the end of the leader is wound to the rod tip, more than one person is permitted to hold the leader, and there is no restriction regarding the use of a gaffer in addition to the persons holding the leader.

5. Rods must be in accordance with sporting ethics and customs. Considerable latitude is allowed, but rods giving the angler an unsporting advantage will be disqualified. The rule is intended to eliminate the use of freak rods, and to act as a means of protection to anglers. The minimum length of the rod tip is 50 inches, and the maximum length of the rod butt is 27 inches. These measurements shall be made from a point directly beneath the center of the reel. A curved butt is measured in a straight line. These limitations do not apply to surf casting rods used in surf casting.

6. Reels must be in accordance with sporting ethics and customs. Mechanical reels of any nature are prohibited. This would include ratchet handle reels, motor, hydraulic or electrically driven reels or any other device giving the angler an unfair advantage. The use of double handled reels is prohibited.

7. Fighting chairs may have no mechanical device which aids the angler in fighting a fish. Gimbals must be free-swinging which also allows a gimbal swinging only in a vertical plane. Any gimbal which allows the angler to reduce strain or to rest while fighting is prohibited.

8. Metal lines, including metal core lines, are prohibited.

9. For bait fishing no more than two single hooks may

be separately attached to the leader or trace, and then only if both hooks are firmly imbedded or attached to the bait. The eyes of the hooks must be at least an overall hook's length apart and no more than 18 inches. A hook's length is the full overall length of the largest of the two hooks. The use of a dangling or swinging hook is prohibited. A so-called "Bottom Rig" for fishing on or close to the bottom is acceptable if it consists of no more than two single hooks on separate leaders with both hooks imbedded in the respective baits and separated sufficiently so that a fish caught on one hook cannot be foul hooked by the other. All claims on two hook tackle must be accompanied by a photograph or sketch of the hook arrangement.

9a. In using a "teaser type" artificial lure with a skirt or trailing material, no more than two single hooks may be separately attached to the leader or trace. The eyes of the hooks must be an overall hook's length apart and no further than 12 inches apart. A hook's length is the full overall length of the largest of the two hooks. The trailing hook may not extend more than a hook's length beyond the skirt of the lure. A photograph showing the hook arrangement must accompany every application.

10. The use of a plug or other artificial lure with gang hooks is permitted. This use shall be limited to a total of two hooks either single, double, treble, or any combination thereof. Hooks must be permanently and directly attached to the lure. All double and treble hooks must be free-swinging. The use of any plug or artificial lure with gang hooks is limited to casting and retrieving in a conventional manner. When casting from a boat, the boat must not be under any form of mechanical propulsion. With

record applications, a photograph of the plug or lure must be submitted, and if it is not completely satisfactory the plug itself may be requested.

11. The use of any float is prohibited other than a small balloon or cork, which may be attached to the line or leader for the sole purpose of regulating the depth of the bait or for drifting of the bait.

12. Entangling devices, either with or without a hook, are prohibited.

13. A gaff not exceeding 8 feet in overall length may be used for boating a fish. In the case of a flying or detachable gaff, the rope may not exceed 30 feet. Only a single, fixed hook is permitted. The gaff rope shall be measured from the point where it is secured to the detachable head to the other end. Only the effective length shall be considered. If a fixed head gaff is used, the same limitations shall apply, and the gaff rope shall be measured from the same location on the gaff hook. No harpoon type attachments are permissible. The gaff length limitation does not apply when fishing from a bridge or pier.

14. The angler must hook, fight, and bring the fish to gaff unaided by any other person. If a rod holder is used and a fish strikes that bait, the angler must remove the rod from the rod holder as quickly as possible. (Note Rule 18C, below.) The intent of this rule is that the angler rather than anyone else should hook and strike the fish.

15. Resting the rod on the gunwale of a boat while playing a fish is prohibited. Harness may be attached to reel or rod. The use of a rod belt is permitted. Replacing or adjusting the harness by another person is permitted.

16. Changing of rod or reel, splicing the line, or removal or addition thereto during the playing of a fish is prohibited.

17. In the event of a multiple strike fought by a single angler, only the first fish fought will be considered for a record.

18. The following acts or omissions will disqualify a catch:

    A. Failure to comply with the rules or tackle specifications.

    B. A broken rod that alters the effective length of the butt or tip beyond limitations or severely impairs the angling characteristics of the rod.

    C. Acts of persons other than the angler in adjusting reel drag or touching any part of the tackle either by hand or other device during the playing of the fish, or giving aid other than taking the leader (or trace) for gaffing purposes.

    D. Handlining or using a handline or rope attached in any manner to a line or leader for the purpose of holding or lifting a fish.

    E. Shooting, harpooning or lancing any fish, including sharks, at any stage of the catch.

    F. Mutilations caused by sharks, other fish or propellers that remove or penetrate the flesh. (Injuries caused by leader or line, scratches, old healed scars and regeneration deformities shall not be considered disqualifying injuries.) Any mutilations on the fish must be explained completely in a separate report accompanying the application.

    G. Chumming with flesh, blood, skin or guts of mammals is prohibited; however, any chumming with whole or parts of fish is permitted providing the chum is allowed to float without restraint. Live chum may be restrained.

H. Beaching or driving into shallow water any fish hooked from a boat, in order to deprive said fish of its normal ability to swim, is prohibited.

19. Only fish caught in accordance with the above rules shall be accepted as record claims by the International Game Fish Association.

Expanded Objectives of the International Game Fish Association

A. Believing that marine sport fish species, related food fish and ocean habitat are economic, social, recreational and aesthetic assets which must be maintained, wisely used and perpetuated for posterity; and believing that the sport of marine game fish angling is an important recreational, economic, and social activity requiring the public to be educated to pursue recreational activities in a manner consistent with sound sporting and conservation practices, the association has dedicated itself to the following objectives.

B. To encourage and further the study of marine game fish angling, the marine species related thereto, and the ocean habitat requirements of such species.

C. To formulate and support fair, uniform and ethical angling rules in order to accumulate angling and game fish resource data.

D. To accumulate and compile marine angling statistics and catch results on a broad basis and to analyze the overall angling effect upon the respective species; to use this information for the formulation of adequate conservation measures to insure the perpetuation of the species and the angling sport.

E. To accumulate and maintain a world-wide history of marine game fishing for the use and benefit of all mankind.

F. To develop and maintain an international library on game fish, the angling sport and related subjects. To make this library a repository for all contributors and to also make the information available to all mankind.

G. To create and maintain a facility where all forms of game-fishing history, papers, statistics, historical articles and artifacts may be accumulated and properly compiled to provide a lasting educational and historical public facility.

H. To develop, promote and support a comprehensive educational program based upon scientific study and marine research for the advancement, perpetuation, wise use, management and conservation of marine game fish species and their natural habitat.

I. To give recognition or awards to any persons for outstanding accomplishments in the field of angling.

J. To analyze pressure of sport fishing and commercial fishing upon the respective game fish species.

K. To act as a data-accumulation center for fishing and results and coordinate such efforts with governments and others by education in the wise use and conservation of the various species.

L. To develop, promote and support the tagging of marine fish in order to compile migration patterns, species growth-rate information and any other pertinent facts, for the use of scientists and ichthyologists in their studies of marine fish species.

M. To develop and maintain a historical film library on

game fish, the angling sport, and the anglers related thereto.

N. To compile scientific and statistical data on the heaviest angling catches for men and women in each line division from 6-pound to 130-pound class on each species recognized and fished for by a substantial amount of anglers or distributed over a wide area of ocean waters. To give recognition to the angler if IGFA ethical sport and conservation rules are adhered to. To publish and distribute all of this information to all members, scientific institutions, marine fish–oriented agencies, marine fish libraries, and recognized authorities and publishers of marine game fish information in all news media.

O. To assist and participate in game fish seminars, symposiums, meetings and gatherings, both domestic and international where the expertise, data, and purposes of this association may be helpful in assisting other organizations having similar objectives in the preservation and wise use of the species.

P. To develop an IGFA fishing publication for all members and clubs that will list all important international fishing news, scientific data related to the species, regular record applications and awards, important member and club activities, results of scientific and game fish meetings and all other matters of importance relating to the conservation and proper management of the species and the preservation and advancement of the sport.

Q. To make grants, fellowships and assistance to game fish–oriented organizations and research institutions for the support of research and the marine sciences related to game fish and the angling sport.

R. In furtherance of the foregoing objectives the associa-

176

tion is impowered to take steps, engage in such activities and cooperation with the local, national, state and international governments and such other agencies including scientific and technical research societies as may be helpful or necessary to these aims.